FRENCH PHRASE BOOK

This phrase book, in a handy pocket size, will help you to be
readily understood on all everyday occasions; to get you,
quickly and easily, *where* you want and *what* you want; and
to enable you to cope with those problems and minor emergencies that always seem to occur on holiday.

A pronunciation guide accompanies each phrase, the topic
of which can quickly be found by reference to the contents
list or the index.

TEACH YOURSELF BOOKS

FRENCH PHRASE BOOK

S. Mungall
and
S. Boas

TEACH YOURSELF BOOKS
Hodder and Stoughton

First printed 1976
Seventh impression 1982

This volume published in the U.S.A. by David McKay Company
Inc., 250 Third Avenue, New York N.Y. 10017.

ISBN 0 340 18260 1

Printed in Great Britain
for Hodder and Stoughton Educational,
a division of Hodder and Stoughton Ltd.,
Mill Road, Dunton Green, Sevenoaks, Kent
by Richard Clay (The Chaucer Press) Ltd,
Bungay, Suffolk

Contents

Using this Phrase Book

In this book we have tried to include all the phrases which you will really need to use when on holiday or travelling in France. Naturally we hope that you will not run into difficulties but, just in case, we have included phrases to cover most of the more common problems and disasters.

The sections are arranged in a logical order and there is a comprehensive index at the back of the book, together with useful reference vocabulary and conversion tables. It does not aim to be a French grammar, but we have presented the most basic elements and you are advised to glance at these before you set out.

One feature which we hope you will find useful is the inclusion of a number of possible answers to most of the questions you will need to ask, except in cases where the obvious answer is 'Yes' or 'No'. In this way, the person to whom you are talking can point to the right answer in the book. Anything a French person is likely to say to you is marked with an asterisk.

Pronunciation Guide

As the book is intended for those with little or no knowledge of French, the scheme of pronunciation which we have used is based on English sounds. It is therefore not completely accurate but it is simple, practical and easy to read. There are several features of French pronunciation which English people may at first find strange:

1 The final consonant of a word is generally not pronounced.

2 There is more or less equal stress on every syllable.

3 Nasal sounds. These have no direct English equivalent and we have described them approximately as follows:

le son (the sound) = le(r) soh(n) (e.g. song without the 'g')
le bain (the bath) = le(r) ba(n)
grand (big) = grah(n)
un (one) = uh(n)

In each case the vowels are pronounced through the nose and the final consonant tends to disappear.

4 The French **j** is pronounced as the final sound in the English word 'leisure'. We have used the symbol 'zh' to indicate this sound.

5 When **gn** come together in a French word they are pronounced in a similar way to the 'ni' in 'onion'. For this sound we have used the symbol 'nj'.

6 The French **u** sound is pronounced in a similar way to the English 'ew' as in 'dew'.

Basic French Grammar

Nouns

ALL nouns in French are either masculine or feminine.

1 The word for 'the' for a masculine noun is **le**
                               for a feminine noun is **la**
                               for a plural noun (masculine of feminine) is **les**

Before a vowel, **le** or **la** is shortened to **l'**.

SINGULAR		PLURAL	
le livre	the book	**les livres**	the books
le(r) leevr		lay leevr	
la maison	the house	**les maisons**	the houses
la mayzoh(n)		lay mayzoh(n)	
l'arbre	the tree	**les arbres**	the trees
larbr		laze arbr*	

The ending of a noun may give a guide to whether it is masculine or feminine (e.g. nouns ending in **-tion** are nearly always feminine), but the only way to be sure is to learn each noun with its gender.
* NB The liaison is often made between 's' at the end of a word and a vowel at the beginning of the next.

2 The word for 'a' for a masculine noun is **un**
                               for a feminine noun is **une**

e.g.   **un livre**   a book
         uh(n) leevr
        une maison   a house
         ewn mayzoh(n)
        un arbre   a tree
         uh(n) narbr

3 In the plural, most nouns in French add **s** (some exceptions are those ending in **s**, **x** and **z**), but this is not usually pronounced.

4 The word for 'some' or 'any' is

for a masculine noun **du**
for a feminine noun **de la**
for a plural noun (masculine or feminine) **des**

Before a vowel, **du** and **de la** are shortened to **de l'**.

5 The word for 'of' is **de** and for 'to' is **à**. These are used as follows, depending on whether the noun is masculine, feminine or plural:

de	**le fils du roi**	the king's son
	le(r) feess dew rwa	
	la porte de la maison	the door of the house
	la port de(r) la mayzoh(n)	
	les pattes de l'animal	the animal's paws
	lay pat de(r) laneemal	
	les pages des livres	the pages of the books
	lay pahzh day leevr	
à	**Je vais au cinéma**	I am going to the cinema
	Zhe(r) vay oh seenaymah	
	Je vais à la maison	I am going to the house
	Zhe(r) vay a la mayzoh(n)	
	Je vais à l'aéroport	I am going to the airport
	Zhe(r) vay a lairopor	
	Je vais aux magasins	I am going to the shops
	Zhe(r) vay oh magaza(n)	

Adjectives

1 Adjective endings depend on whether a noun is masculine, feminine or plural. As a general rule, you add an **e** to make an adjective feminine and an **s** to make it plural.

The word for 'little' is **petit**:

e.g.   **le petit livre**   the little book
        le(r) pe(r)tee leevr
        la petite maison   the little house
        la pe(r)teet mayzoh(n)
        les petits livres   the little books
        lay pe(r)tee leevr
        les petites maisons   the little houses
        lay pe(r)teet mayzoh(n)

There is a list of useful adjectives on p. 13.

2 'This' and 'that', 'these' and 'those' are as follows:

ce livre	this *or* that book	**ces livres**	these *or* those books
se(r) leevr		say leevr	
cette maison	this *or* that house	**ces maisons**	these *or* those houses
set mayzoh(n)		say mayzoh(n)	
cet arbre	this *or* that tree	**ces arbres**	these *or* those trees
set arbr		sayz arbr	

3 The word for 'my', 'his', 'your', etc. depends on whether the noun it refers to is masculine, feminine or plural.

	MASCULINE	FEMININE	PLURAL
my	**mon**	**ma**	**mes**
	moh(n)	ma	may
your	**ton**	**ta**	**tes**
(*familiar*)	toh(n)	ta	tay
his, her, its	**son**	**sa**	**ses**
	soh(n)	sa	say
our	**notre**	**notre**	**nos**
	notr	notr	noh
your	**votre**	**votre**	**vos**
	votr	votr	voh
their	**leur**	**leur**	**leurs**
	ler	ler	ler

e.g.	**mon livre**	my book	**mes parents**	my parents
	moh(n) leevr		may parah(n)	
	sa maison	his (*or* her) house	**ses mains**	his hands
	sa mayzoh(n)		say ma(n)	
	notre fille	our daughter	**nos fils**	our sons
	notr fee		noh feess	
	vos lampes	your lamps	**votre chien**	your dog
	voh lah(n)p		votr shya(n)	
	leur arbre	their tree	**leurs jardins**	their gardens
	ler arbr		ler zharda(n)	

Pronouns

je	I	**nous**	we
zhe(r)		noo	
tu	you*	**vous**	you
tew		voo	
il	he (it)	**ils**	they (*m.*)
eel		eel	
elle	she (it)	**elles**	they (*f.*)
el		el	

It is very common in French to use the word **on**, meaning 'one', 'people', 'we', etc.

e.g.	**On va manger maintenant**	We are going to eat now
	Oh(n) va mah(n)zhay ma(n) tenah(n)	
	On boit du vin en France	People drink wine in France
	Oh(n) bwa dew va(n) ah(n) Frah(n)ss	

* The form **tu** is only used for children and close friends so when addressing someone you should generally use the form **vous**.

Verbs

The verbs 'to be' and 'to have' are formed as follows:

être *to be*
etr

avoir *to have*
avwahr

je suis	I am	**j'ai**	I have
zhe(r) swee		zhay	
tu es	you are	**tu as**	you have
tew ay		tew a	
il est	he (it) is	**il a**	he has
eel ay		eel a	
elle est	she (it) is	**elle a**	she has
el ay		el a	
nous sommes	we are	**nous avons**	we have
noo som		noo zavoh(n)	
vous êtes	you are	**vous avez**	you have
voo zet		voo zavay	
ils sont	they are (*m.*)	**ils ont**	they have (*m.*)
eel soh(n)		eel zoh(n)	
elles sont	they are (*f.*)	**elles ont**	they have (*f.*)
el soh(n)		el zoh(n)	

Most French verbs correspond to one of three patterns.

1 Verbs ending in -er, e.g. **parler** 'to speak'

je parle	I speak	**nous parlons**	we speak
zhe(r) parl		noo parloh(n)	
tu parles	you speak	**vous parlez**	you speak
tew parl		voo parlay	
il/elle parle	he/she speaks	**ils/elles parlent**	they speak
eel/el parl		eel/el parl	

2 Verbs ending in -ir, e.g. **finir** 'to finish'

je finis zhe(r) feenee	I finish	**nous finissons** noo feeneessoh(n)	we finish
tu finis tew feenee	you finish	**vous finissez** voo feeneessay	you finish
il/elle finit eel/el feenee	he/she finishes	**ils/elles finissent** eel/el feeneess	they finish

3 Verbs ending in -re, e.g. **vendre** 'to sell'

je vends zhe(r) vah(n)	I sell	**nous vendons** noo vah(n)doh(n)	we sell
tu vends tew vah(n)	you sell	**vous vendez** voo vah(n)day	you sell
il/elle vend eel/el vah(n)	he/she sells	**ils/elles vendent** eel/el vah(n)d	they sell

Here are some useful irregular verbs:

aller *to go*
allay

je vais zhe(r) vay	I go	**nous allons** noo zalloh(n)	we go
tu vas tew va	you go	**vous allez** voo zallay	you go
il/elle va eel/el va	he/she goes	**ils/elles vont** eel/el voh(n)	they go

devoir *to have to*
de(r)vwahr

je dois zhe(r) dwa	I must	**nous devons** noo de(r)voh(n)	we must
tu dois tew dwa	you must	**vous devez** voo de(r)vay	you must
il/elle doit eel/el dwa	he/she must	**ils/elles doivent** eel/el dwav	they must

faire to do, make
fair

je fais	I do	**nous faisons**	we do
zhe(r) fay		noo fe(r)zoh(n)	
tu fais	you do	**vous faites**	you do
tew fay		voo fet	
il/elle fait	he/she does	**ils/elles font**	they do
eel/el fay		eel/el foh(n)	

pouvoir to be able
poovwahr

je peux	I can	**nous pouvons**	we can
zhe(r) pe(r)		noo poovoh(n)	
tu peux	you can	**vous pouvez**	you can
tew pe(r)		voo poovay	
il/elle peut	he/she can	**ils/elles peuvent**	they can
eel/el pe(r)		eel/el pe(r)v	

venir to come
ve(r)neer

je viens	I come	**nous venons**	we come
zhe(r) vya(n)		noo ve(r)noh(n)	
tu viens	you come	**vous venez**	you come
tew vya(n)		voo ve(r)nay	
il/elle vient	he/she comes	**ils/elles viennent**	they come
eel/el vya(n)		eel/el vyen	

vouloir to want (to)
voolwahr

je veux	I want	**nous voulons**	we want
zhe(r) ve(r)		noo vooloh(n)	
tu veux	you want	**vous voulez**	you want
tew ve(r)		voo voolay	
il/elle veut	he/she wants	**ils/elles veulent**	they want
eel/el ve(r)		eel/el ve(r)l	

The negative of a verb is formed by adding **ne** before the verb and **pas** after it.

e.g.   **Je ne vais pas**   **Vous ne devez pas**
         Zhe(r) ne(r) vay pah   Voo ne(r) de(r)vay pah

To ask a question, you can either put the verb first

e.g.   **voulez-vous?**   do you want?
         voolay-voo?
         parlez-vous anglais?   do you speak English?
         parlay-voo ah(n)glay?

or use the phrase **est-ce que**

e.g.   **est-ce que vous voulez?**
         esske(r) voo voolay?
         est-ce que vous parlez anglais?
         esske(r) voo parlay ah(n)glay?

Everyday Words and Expressions

Essentials

Yes	**Oui**	Wee
No	**Non**	Noh(n)
Please	**S'il vous plaît**	Seelvooplay
Thank you	**Merci**	Mairssee

Greetings, farewells, apologies

When you meet someone in France you say **Bonjour** (Good morning *or* Good afternoon). It is considered polite always to address a man as **Monsieur** and a woman as **Madame** or **Mademoiselle**:

e.g. **Bonjour, monsieur**   Good morning *or* good afternoon
Pardon, madame   I'm sorry, excuse me
Au revoir, mademoiselle   Goodbye

A man is always addressed as **Monsieur** whatever his age or status.

An adult woman is **Madame** unless you know she is not married, in which case you may use **Mademoiselle**.

Young girls, waitresses, telephone operators, etc. are addressed as **Mademoiselle**.

When you are introduced to someone or meet someone (whether for the first time or not) you shake hands. The French shake hands far more often than we do, both on arrival and on departure.

If someone introduces you to someone else, say **Enchanté, monsieur/madame/mademoiselle,** which is the equivalent of 'Pleased to meet you'.

Greetings

Good morning/Good afternoon.	**Bonjour (monsieur, madame, mademoiselle).** Boh(n)zhoor (me(r)syer, mahdahm, mamwazel).
Good evening.	**Bonsoir.** Boh(n)swahr.
Hullo!	**Salut!** Salew!
How are you?	**Comment allez-vous?** Comah(n)tallay-voo?
Not too bad, thank you.	**Ça va, merci.** Sa va, mairssee.
Very well, thank you.	**Très bien, merci.** Tray byah(n), mairssee.
This is my wife/husband.	**Je vous présente ma femme/ mon mari.** Zhe(r) voo prayzeh(n)t ma fahm/ moh(n) maree.
Delighted.	**Enchanté.** Ah(n)shah(n)tay.
My name is. . . .	**Je m'appelle. . . .** Zhe(r) mappell. . . .

Farewells

Goodbye.	**Au revoir.** Oh re(r)vwahr.
Good night.	**Bonne nuit.** Bon-nwee.
See you later.	**A toute à l'heure.** A toota ler.
See you soon.	**A bientôt.** A byah(n)toh.
Till tomorrow.	**A demain.** A dema(n).

Apologies

I'm sorry.	**Pardon.**
	Pahrdoh(n).
Excuse me!	**Excusez-moi!**
	Excuzay-mwa!
Don't mention it.	**Je vous en prie.**
	Zhe(r) voozah(n) pree.

Simple questions

Can I have . . .?	**Puis-je avoir . . .?**
	Pwee zhavwahr . . .?
Can you show me . . .?	**Pouvez-vous me montrer?**
	Poovay-voo me(r) montray?
Can you help me?	**Pouvez-vous m'aider?**
	Poovay-voo medday?
Do you have any . . .?	**Avez-vous des . . .?**
	Avay-voo day . . .?
How much/how many?	**Combien?**
	Combya(n)?
How many times?	**Combien de fois?**
	Combya(n) de(r) fwa?
How long?	**Combien de temps?**
	Combya(n) de(r) tah(n)
Is that . . .?	**Est-ce que c'est . . .?**
	Esskersay . . .?
Is there/are there . . .?	**Y a-t-il . . .?**
	Yateel . . .?
*There is/are.	**Il y a.**
	Eelya.
*There isn't/aren't.	**Il n'y a pas.**
	Eel nyapah.
What is that?	**Qu'est-ce que c'est?**
	Kesskersay?
*It's a. . . .	**C'est un. . . .**
	Saytuh(n). . . .

What do you want? **Que voulez-vous?**
Ke(r) voolay-voo?

What's the matter? **Qu'est-ce qu'il y a?**
Kesskeelya?

What does that mean? **Qu'est-ce que cela veut dire?**
Kesske(r) sla ve(r) deer?

What is your name? **Comment vous appelez-vous?**
Comah(n) voozapplay-voo?

What is the time? **Quelle heure est-il?**
Kel er eteel?

When? **Quand?**
Kah(n)?

Where? **Où?**
Oo?

Where is/are . . .? **Où est/sont . . .?**
Oo ay/soh(n) . . .?

*It is. . . . **Il est. . . .**
Eel ay. . . .

*They are. . . . **Ils sont. . . .**
Eel soh(n). . . .

Where can I find a . . .? **Où puis-je trouver un . . .?**
Oo pwee-zhe(r) troovay uh(n) . . .?

*Here it is. **Le voici.**
Le(r) vwassee.

*Here they are. **Les voici.**
Lay vwassee.

Who? **Qui?**
Kee?

Who should I ask? **A qui faut-il s'adresser?**
A kee foh-teel saddressay?

Why? **Pourquoi?**
Porkwa?

Why not? **Pourquoi pas?**
Porkwa pah?

Simple descriptions

It is good.	**C'est bon.** Say boh(n).
They are good.	**Ils sont bons.** Eel soh(n) boh(n).
It is very good.	**C'est très bon.** Say tray boh(n).
It is not good.	**Ce n'est pas bon.** Snay pay boh(n).
It is....	**C'est....** Say....
bad	**mauvais** mohvay
better	**meilleur** mayer
big	**grand** grah(n)
cheap	**bon marché** boh(n) marshay
cold	**froid** frwa
difficult	**difficile** diffiseel
early	**tôt** toh
easy	**facile** faseel
empty	**vide** veed
expensive	**cher** share
far	**loin** lwa(n)
free	**libre** leebr
funny	**amusant** amuzah(n)
full	**plein** pla(n)
hard	**dur** dewr
heavy	**lourd** loor
here	**ici** eessee
high	**haut** oh
hot	**chaud** shoh
low	**bas** bah
last	**dernier** dernyay
late	**tard** tar
light (weight)	**léger** layzhay
near	**près** pray
new	**nouveau** noovoh
next	**prochain** prosha(n)
occupied	**occupé** occupay
old	**vieux** vye(r)
open	**ouvert** oovair
right (correct)	**juste** zhyoost

serious	**grave**	grahv
shut	**fermé**	fairmay
small	**petit**	pe(r)tee
soft	**mou**	moo
stupid	**stupide**	stewpeed
there	**là**	lah
ugly	**laid**	lay
worse	**pire**	peer
wrong	**faux**	foh

Miscellaneous useful phrases

I can't.	**Je ne peux pas.** Zhe(r) ne(r) pe(r) pah.
I'm hungry.	**J'ai faim.** Zhay fa(n).
I'm in a hurry.	**Je suis pressé.** Zhe(r) swee pressay.
I know.	**Je le sais.** Zhe(r) le say.
I don't know.	**Je ne sais pas.** Zhe(r) ne(r) say pah.
I like that.	**J'aime ça.** Zhem sa.
I don't like that.	**Je n'aime pas ça.** Zhe(r) nem pah sa.
I would like....	**Je voudrais....** Zhe(r) voodray....
I'm lost.	**Je suis perdu.** Zhe(r) swee pairdew.
It doesn't matter.	**Ça ne fait rien.** Sa ne(r) fay rya(n).
I'm tired.	**Je suis fatigué.** Zhe(r) swee fateegay.

Simple exclamations

Come in!	**Entrez!** Ah(n)tray!
Come here!	**Venez ici!** Venay zeessee!
Go away!	**Allez-vous-en!** Allay-voozah(n)!
Very good!	**Très bien!** Tray bya(n)!
Help!	**Au secours!** Oh scoor!
Idiot!	**Idiot!** Eedyoh!
Listen!	**Écoutez!** Aycootay!
Quick!	**Vite!** Veet!
Stop!	**Arrêtez-vous!** Arretay-voo!
Stop thief!	**Au voleur!** Oh voler!
Too bad!	**Tant pis!** Tah(n) pee!
What a pity!	**Quel dommage!** Kel doma(r)zh!

Miscellaneous signs and notices

Arrêtez	Stop
Ascenseur	Lift
Chaud	Hot
Chambres à louer	Rooms to let
Chien méchant	Beware of the dog
Complet	Full
Dames	Ladies

Danger de mort	Danger of death
Défense d'afficher	No bill sticking
Défense de cracher	No spitting
Défense de fumer	No smoking
Eau non potable	Not drinking water
Eau potable	Drinking water
Entrée	Entrance
Entrée gratuite	Entrance free
Entrée interdite	No entrance
Fermé	Closed
Fermeture annuelle	Closed for holidays
Frappez	Knock
Froid	Cold
Issue de secours	Emergency exit
Libre	Free
Messieurs	Gentlemen
Occupé	Engaged
Ouvert	Open
Poussez	Push
Privé	Private
Propriété privée	Private property
Renseignements	Information
Réservé	Reserved
Sonnez	Ring
Sortie	Exit
Tirez	Pull
Toilettes	Toilets

Linguistic problems

I am English.

Je suis Anglais/Anglaise.
Zhe(r) sweez ah(n)glay/
ah(n)glayse.

Do you speak English?

Parlez-vous anglais?
Pahrlay-voo zah(n)glay?

I only speak English.	**Je ne parle que l'anglais.**
	Zhe(r) ne(r) pahrl ke(r) lah(n)glay.
I don't speak French.	**Je ne parle pas français.**
	Zhe(r) ne(r) pahrl pah frah(n)say.
I don't understand.	**Je ne comprends pas.**
	Zhe(r) ne(r) coh(m)prah(n) pah.
Is there anyone here who speaks English?	**Y a-t-il quelqu'un ici qui parle anglais?**
	Yateel kelkuh(n) eessee kee pahrl ah(n)glay?
Please write it down.	**Voulez-vous l'écrire, s'il vous plaît?**
	Voolay-voo laycreer, seelvooplay?
Please point to the answer.	**Voulez-vous désigner votre réponse du doigt?**
	Voolay-voo dayseenyay votr raypoh(n)s dew dwa?
Please speak slowly.	**Lentement, s'il vous plaît.**
	Lah(n)tmah(n), seelvooplay.
Please repeat that.	**Voulez-vous répéter cela, s'il vous plaît?**
	Voolay-voo raypaytay sla, seelvooplay?
Could you translate this, please?	**Voulez-vous traduire cela, s'il vous plaît?**
	Voolay-voo tradweer sla, seelvooplay?

Directions

Can you tell me the way to . . . ?	**Pourriez-vous m'indiquer le chemin pour . . . ?**
	Pooryay-voo ma(n)deekay le(r) she(r)ma(n) poor . . . ?

How do I get to the church?
L'église, s'il vous plaît?
Laygleez, seelvooplay?

I am lost.
Je suis perdu.
Zhe(r) swee pairdew

I am looking for....
Je cherche....
Zhe(r) shairsh....

*Go straight ahead.
Continuez tout droit.
Continuay too drwa.

*Turn right/left.
Tournez à droite/à gauche.
Tournay a drwaht/a gohsh.

*Take the first turn on the right/
   on the left.
**Prenez le premier à droite/à
   gauche.**
Prenay le(r) premyay a drwaht/
   a gohsh.

*Go past the church/bridge/
   post-office/lights.
**Continuez au-delà de l'église/
   du pont/du bureau de poste/
   des feux.**
Continuay ohdla de(r) laygleez/
   du poh(n)/ dew buro de(r) post/
   day fe(r).

*Just before the roundabout.
Juste avant le rond-point.
Zhust avah(n) le(r) roh(n)pwah(n).

*Just after the bridge.
Juste après le pont.
Zhust apray le(r) poh(ŋ).

Is it far?
C'est loin?
Say lwah(n)?

*It is five/ten minutes walk.
C'est à cinq/dix minutes à pied.
Say a sank/dee meenewt a pyay.

*It is too far to walk.
C'est trop loin pour aller à pied.
Say troh lwah(n) poor allay a
   pyay.

*You should take the bus/train/
   metro.
**Vous devriez prendre l'autobus/
   le train/ le métro.**
Voo devryay prah(n)dr lohtobus/
   le(r) tra(n)/le(r) metro.

Please show me on the map.

Voulez-vous m'indiquer sur la carte?

Voolay-voo ma(n)dikay soor la cart?

*Over here/over there.

Là-bas.

Lah-bah.

*This way/that way.

Par ici/par là.

Pahr eessee/pahr lah.

The Customs

Day-trippers to France no longer need a passport, but if you are staying overnight you must take a valid passport with you. This is the only document you need unless you are taking the car, in which case various other documents are also necessary. (See section on 'Travelling by car', p. 21.)

When you arrive in France you have to go through Passport Control and Customs (**La Douane**), where there is certain to be someone who speaks English. Customs officials are usually eager to let you through as quickly as possible.

*Your passport, please.
: **Votre passeport, s'il vous plaît.**
  Votr passpor, seelvooplay.

*Have you anything to declare?
: **Avez-vous quelque chose à déclarer?**
  Avay-voo kelkeshohs a declaray?

I have nothing to declare.
: **Je n'ai rien à déclarer.**
  Zhe(r) nay ryah(n) a declaray.

Must I pay on these things?
: **Faut-il payer pour ces choses?**
  Foht-eel payay poor say shohz?

I have lost my passport.
: **J'ai perdu mon passeport.**
  Zhay pairdu moh(n) passpor.

Travelling by car

To motor in France you need the following documents: passport, green card, registration book, valid driving licence. If you are taking a trailer or caravan, you will need a **carnet de passage en douane** (Customs transit permit). You should display a nationality plate, and it is advisable to use amber-coloured bulbs or converters for your headlights, and have them altered to dip to the left. You should also carry a red warning triangle in case of accident or breakdown.

In all continental countries, driving is on the right. You may not park when there is a continuous line in the centre of the road. In some built-up areas, parking is allowed on one side of the road for part of the month and on the other side for the rest of the month. Large towns have blue parking zones. Discs, obtainable from tourist offices, tobacco kiosks and garages, should be displayed on your windscreen. Failure to comply with this may lead to a fine or your car being towed away.

There are four grades of road in France:

Autoroutes (A) motorways, the majority of which charge a toll
Routes nationales (N) main roads
Routes départementales (D) 'B' roads
Chemins vicinaux (V) local or side roads

For general directions on 'how to get there', please look at pp. 17–18.

How do I get to ...	Où se trouve ...
	Oo se(r) troov ...
– the motorway?	– l'autoroute?
	– lohtoroute?
– the scenic route to Nîmes?	– la route touristique de Nîmes?
	– la route touristic de(r) Neem?

– the main road to Calais?	**– la grande route de Calais?** – la grah(n)d route de(r) Calay?
Where is the nearest car park?	**Où est le parking le plus proche?** Oo ay le(r) parking le(r) plew prosh?
Can I park here?	**Puis-je stationner ici?** Pweezh stassyonay eessee?
How long can I leave the car here?	**Combien de temps puis-je laisser la voiture ici?** Combya(n) de(r) tah(n) pweezh lessay la vwatew eessee?
Do I need lights?	**Dois-je allumer mes phares?** Dwazh allewmay may far?
How far is the nearest service station?	**Où se trouve la station-service la plus proche?** Oo se(r) troov la stassyoh(n)-sairveess la plew prosh?
Where is the nearest garage?	**Où est le garage le plus proche?** Oo ay le(r) garahzh le(r) plew prosh?

At the service station

Ten francs' worth of petrol, please.	**Donnez-moi dix francs de l'essence, s'il vous plaît.** Donnay-mwa dee frah(n) de(r) lessah(n)ss seelvooplay.
Twenty litres of regular/super.	**Vingt litres de normale/super.** Va(n) leetr de(r) normahl/soopair.
Fill the tank up, please.	**Faites-moi le plein d'essence, s'il vous plaît.** Fet-mwa le(r) pla(n) dessah(n)ss seelvooplay.
Please check the oil/the water/the tyres.	**Vérifiez l'huile/l'eau/les pneus, s'il vous plaît.** Verifyay lweel/loh/lay ne(r), seelvooplay.

Please change the oil/this tyre.	**Changez l'huile/ce pneu, s'il vous plaît.**
	Shah(n)zhay lweel/se(r) ne(r), seelvooplay.
Do you sell maps of the area?	**Est-ce que vous vendez des cartes de la région?**
	Esske(r) voo vah(n)day day cart de(r) la rayzhon?
Are there any toilets here?	**Y a-t-il des toilettes ici?**
	Yateel day twalet eessee?

COMMON ROAD SIGNS

Accès difficile aux autos	Access difficult for cars
Allumez vos phares	Switch your headlights on
Attention: travaux sur 10 km	Roadworks for 10 km: drive with care
Attention: sortie de camions	Danger: lorries turning
Centre ville	Town centre
Chaussée déformée	Damaged road surface
Déviation	Diversion
Hauteur limitée à ...	Vehicles under ... in height only
(Fin d')Interdiction de doubler	(End of) No overtaking
Interdit aux poids lourds	No heavy vehicles
Passage à niveau	Level crossing
Passage protégé	Priority to vehicles on main road
Piétons: attendez	Pedestrians: wait
passez	cross
Poste suivant à 50 km	Next roadside phone 50 km
Priorité à droite	Priority to the right
Ralentir	Slow down
Sens interdit	No entry
Sens unique	One-way street
Serrez à droite	Keep right
Stationnement interdit les jours pairs/impairs	No parking on even/odd days

Stationnement autorisé	Parking allowed
Point noir	Black spot
Tenez votre gauche	Keep to your left
Toutes directions	All directions
Verglas	Black ice
Virages sur 2 km	Bends for 2 km
Zone bleue	Blue-zone parking

Breakdowns

Service stations do not handle major repairs. On autoroutes there are roadside phone boxes every 2.4 kilometres. These are connected to police stations, who will contact a garage for you. Any repairs must be paid for on the spot, so you are advised to be fully insured.

There is often no petrol, repairs or breakdown service on Sundays and public holidays (see list at the back of the book). The Touring-Club de France has a breakdown service. Information on membership is obtainable from the AA or RAC. For further information on affiliation with motoring clubs, you should contact:

> Automobile-Club de France,
> 6, Place de la Concorde,
> Paris 75008

or

> Touring-Club de France,
> 65 avenue de la Grande-Armee,
> Paris 75016

See the section on 'Accidents and Emergencies' for what to do if you are involved in an accident.

I have broken down.

Je suis en panne.
Zhe(r) swee ah(n) pan.

Please can you let me have a can of petrol?

Pourriez-vous me donner un bidon d'essence, s'il vous plaît?
Poorryay-voo me(r) donay uh(n) beedoh(n) dessah(n)ss, seelvooplay?

My car has broken down. Could you drive me to the nearest garage?

Ma voiture est en panne. Pourriez-vous me conduire au garage le plus proche?
Ma vwatrew aytah(n) pan. Poorryay-voo me(r) coh(n)dweer oh garahzh le(r) plew prosh?

May I use your telephone?

Puis-je me servir de votre téléphone?
Pweezh me(r) sairveer de(r) votr taylayphon?

Is there a breakdown service at this garage?

Est-ce que ce garage a un service de dépannage?
Esske(r) se(r) garahzh a uh(n) sairveess de(r) daypanahzh?

I have broken down 2 kilometres from here.

Je suis en panne à deux kilomètres d'ici.
Zhe(r) swee ah(n) pan a de(r) kilometr deessee.

Can you send a mechanic?

Pouvez-vous envoyer un mécanicien?
Poovay-voo ah(n)vwayay uh(n) maycaneessyah(n)?

Could you send a breakdown lorry to tow my car to the garage?

Pourriez-vous envoyer une dépanneuse pour remorquer ma voiture au garage?
Pooryay-voo ah(n)vwayay ewn daypane(r)z poor remorkay ma vwatewr oh garahzh?

At the garage

What time does this garage open/close?	**A quelle heure ouvre/ferme ce garage?** A kel er oovr/fairm se(r) garahzh?
Is there a mechanic here?	**Y a-t-il un mécanicien ici?** Yateel uh(n) maycaneessyah(n) eessee?
There is something wrong with my car.	**Ma voiture ne marche pas bien.** Ma vwatewr ne(r) marsh pah bya(n).
*What's the trouble?	**Qu'est-ce qui ne va pas?** Kesskee ne(r) va pah?

Some common symptoms

There is a strange noise/knocking/grating (squeak) in the engine.	**Il y a un bruit étrange/un cognement/un grincement/dans le moteur.** Eelya uh(n) brwee aytrah(n)zh/uh(n) coh(n)jmah(n)/uh(n) gra(n)ssmah(n)/dah(n) le(r) moter.
The car smells of petrol/oil/burning rubber.	**La voiture sent/l'essence/l'huile/le caoutchouc brûlé.** La vwatewr sah(n) lessah(n)ss/lweel/le(r) caooshoo brewlay.
The engine is stalling/misfiring/overheating/frozen.	**Le moteur câle/a des râtés/chauffe trop/est gelé.** Le(r) moter cal/a day ratay/shohf troh/ay gelay.
The engine has seized up.	**Le moteur est grippé.** Le(r) moter ay greepay.
The steering is slack.	**La direction a du jeu.** La deereksyoh(n) a dew je(r).
The steering wheel is vibrating.	**Le volant vibre.** Le(r) volah(n) veebr.

The clutch is jammed/slipping.	**L'embrayage est coincé/patine.** Lah(n)brayazh ay cwa(n)say/ pateen.
The accelerator pedal is loose.	**La pédale d'accélération a du jeu.** La paydal daksaylayrassyoh(n) a dew zhe(r).
The gear lever is stiff.	**Le levier de changement de vitesse est dur.** Le(r) levyay de(r) shah(n)zhmah(n) de(r) veetess ay dure.
The radiator is leaking/steaming.	**Le radiateur a une fuite/fume.** Le(r) radyater a ewn fweet/fume.
The . . . is not working.	**Le . . . ne fonctionne pas.** Le(r) . . . ne(r) foh(n)ksyon pah.
– starter	**– démarreur** – daymarrer
– choke	**– starter** – startair
– horn	**– klaxon** – klaxoh(n)
– heating	**– chauffage** – shohfahzh
– hand-brake	**– frein à main** – fra(n) a ma(n)
The brakes/headlights/indicators are not working.	**Les freins/phares/clignotants ne fonctionnent pas.** Lay fra(n)/far/cleenyotah(n) ne(r) foh(n)ksyon pah.
The exhaust pipe is loose.	**Le tuyau d'échappement n'est plus fixé.** Le(r) tweeyoh dayshapmoh(n) nay plew feexay.
I have lost the ignition key.	**J'ai perdu la clef de contact.** Zhay pairdew la clay de(r) coh(n)tac.
The lock is broken/jammed.	**La serrure est cassée/bloquée.** La serrewr ay cassay/blockay.

Travelling by train

The various types of train in France are:

Le rapide   fast, long-distance express stopping at major stations only
L'express   fairly fast, long-distance stopping train
L'omnibus   slow train stopping at all stations
L'autorail   light diesel train

There is also the TEE (Trans-European Express), which provides a very fast inter-continental service for a supplementary fare.

Children under four travel free on the French railway, and children under ten pay half-fare. For details of other reductions (tourist tickets etc.), contact the French Railways Ltd, 178 Piccadilly, London W1R 0EN.

It is always advisable to book seats in advance. Breakfast, lunch and dinner are provided on all principal trains and can also be booked in advance. Other trains may include a buffet car, or an attendant may come round selling snacks and drinks from a trolley.

Wagon-lits (sleeping-car compartments) or couchettes (berths with pillow and blanket) are available on principal trains and should be reserved in advance if possible.

Where is . . .   Où est . . .
                                    Oo ay . . .
– the station?   – la gare?
                                    – la gar?
– the ticket office?   – le guichet?
                                    – le(r) geeshay?
– the information office?   – le bureau des renseignements?
                                    – le(r) buro day
                                       rah(n)ssennjmah(n)?

– the reservations office?   – **le bureau des réservations?**
    – le(r) buro day
      raysairvassyoh(n)?

– the left luggage office?   – **la consigne?**
    – la coh(n)seenj?

– the lost property office?   – **le bureau des objets trouvés?**
    – le(r) buro daze obzhay
      troovay?

– the waiting room?   – **la salle d'attente?**
    – la sal dattah(n)t?

– platform 3?   – **le quai numéro trois?**
    – le(r) kay newmairoh trwa?

*Over there.   **Là-bas.**
    Labah.

*On the right/left.   **A droite/gauche.**
    A drwat/gohsh.

*Upstairs.   **En haut.**
    Ah(n) oh.

*Downstairs.   **En bas.**
    Ah(n) bah.

Enquiries

Is there a through train for ...?   **Y a-t-il un train direct pour ...?**
    Yateel uh(n) tra(n) deerect
      poor ...?

Where do I have to change?   **Où dois-je changer de train?**
    Oo dwazh shah(n)zhay de(r)
      tra(n)?

What time does the connection to   **A quelle heure part la**
... leave?   **correspondance pour ...?**
    A kel er par la
      correspoh(n)dah(n)ss poor ...?

What time does the train leave?   **A quelle heure part le train?**
    A kel er par le(r) tra(n)?

What time does it get to Calais?	**A quelle heure arrive-t-il à Calais?**
	A kel er arreev-teel a Calay?
Which platform does the train leave from?	**De quelle voie part le train?**
	De(r) kel vwa par le(r) tra(n)?
Does the train stop at . . . ?	**Est-ce que le train s'arrête à . . . ?**
	Esske(r) le(r) tra(n) sarret a . . . ?
When does the next/last train for Paris leave?	**A quelle heure part le prochain/ dernier train pour Paris?**
	A kel er par le(r) prosha(n)/ dairnyay tra(n) poor Paree?
Is it an express/a fast train/ a stopping train?	**Est-ce un rapide/ un express/ un omnibus?**
	Ess uh(n) rapeed/uhnexpress/ uhnomneebooss?
How long is the journey?	**Combien de temps dure le voyage?**
	Combya(n) de(r) tah(n) dewr le(r) vwayahzh?
Is there a dining-car/buffet on the train?	**Y a-t-il un wagon-restaurant/ buffet dans le train?**
	Yateel uh(n) vagoh(n)- restorah(n)/bewfay dah(n) le(r) tra(n)?
Is there a sleeping-car on the train?	**Y a-t-il un wagon-lit dans le train?**
	Yateel uh(n) vagoh(n)-lee dah(n) le(r) tra(n)?
I would like to register my luggage.	**Je voudrais enregistrer mes bagages.**
	Zhe(r) voodray ah(n)rayzheestray may bagahzh.
Do you have a timetable, please?	**Avez-vous un horaire de SNCF, s'il vous plaît?**
	Avay-voo uhnorair de(r) ess-en-say-eff, seelvooplay?

Tickets

I would like a single ticket/a return ticket to. . . .

Je voudrais un billet simple/un billet aller et retour à. . . .

Zhe(r) voodray uh(n) beeyay sah(n)pl/uh(n) beeyay allay ay retor a. . . .

Three singles to Nantes.

Trois aller Nantes.

Trwazallay Nah(n)t.

Two seats on the 4.30 to Dijon, please.

Deux places dans le train de quatre heures et demi pour Dijon, s'il vous plaît.

De(r) plass dah(n) le(r) tra(n) de(r) katrer ay demee poor Deezhoh(n), seelvooplay.

I would like to reserve a seat on the train to Bordeaux tomorrow morning.

Je voudrais réserver une place pour Bordeaux dans le train de demain matin.

Zhe(r) voodray raysairvay ewn plass poor Bordoh dah(n) le(r) tra(n) de(r) dema(n) matah(n).

What is the fare to . . . ?

Quel est le tarif pour . . . ?

Kel ay le(r) tareef poor . . . ?

What is the fare for a child?

Quel est le tarif pour un enfant?

Kel ay le(r) tareef poor uhnah(n)fah(n)?

A smoker.

Un fumeur.

Uh(n) fewmer.

A non-smoker.

Un non-fumeur.

Uh(n) noh(n)-fewmer.

Can I reserve a compartment in the sleeping-car?

Puis-je réserver un compartiment dans le wagon-lit?

Pweezh raysairvay uh(n) comparteemah(n) dah(n) le(r) vagoh(n)-lee?

How much are the couchettes?

Combien sont les couchettes?

Combya(n) soh(n) lay coushet?

On the platform

Is this the train to Marseille?

C'est bien le train pour Marseille?
Say bya(n) le(r) tra(n) poor Marsay?

*Yes, but this carriage stops at....

Oui, mais ce wagon-ci s'arrête à....
Wee, may se(r) vagoh(n)-see sarret a....

*The first two carriages are going to Marseille.

Les deux premiers wagons vont jusqu'à Marseille.
Lay de(r) premyay vagoh(n) voh(n) zhooska Marsay.

*No, the Marseille train is at platform 5.

Non, le train pour Marseille est au quai numéro cinq.
Noh(n) le(r) tra(n) poor Marsay etoh kay newmairoh sank.

On the train

Is this seat free?

Cette place est-elle libre?
Set plass ettell leebr?

Excuse me, that's my seat.

Pardonnez-moi, cette place est à moi.
Pardonnay-mwa, set plass ettamwa.

*The whole compartment is reserved.

Tout le compartiment est réservé.
Too le(r) coh(n)parteemah(n) ay raysairvay.

Do you mind if ...

Vous permettez que ...
Voo pairmettay ke(r) ...

– I open the window?

– j'ouvre la fenêtre?
– zhoovr la fenetr?

– I close the window?

– je ferme la fenêtre?
– zhe(r) fairm la fenetr?

– I turn the heating down?

– je baisse le chauffage?
– zhe(r) bess le(r) shohfahzh?

– I turn the heating up?
– **je hausse le chauffage?**
– zhe(r) ohss le(r) shohfahzh?

– I close the door?
– **je ferme la portière?**
– zhe(r) fairm la portyair?

– I turn the light off?
– **j'éteigne la lumière?**
– zhaytenj la lewmyair?

– I turn the light on?
– **j'allume?**
– zhallewm?

– I draw the curtain?
– **je tire le rideau?**
– zhe(r) teer le(r) reedoh?

– I put your case in the corridor?
– **je mette votre valise dans le couloir?**
– zhe(r) met votr valeez dah(n) le(r) coolwahr?

Excuse me, but this is a non-smoker.
Excusez-moi, mais ce compartiment est un non-fumeur.
Ekskyouzay-mwa, may se(r) comparteemah(n) ay tuh(n) noh(n)-fewmer.

I have left my ticket/passport in the compartment.
J'ai laissé mon billet/passeport dans le compartiment.
Zhay laysay moh(n) beeyay/ passpor dah(n) le(r) comparteemah(n).

The group leader has our tickets.
Le chef du groupe a les billets.
Le(r) shef dew group a lay beeyay.

What station is this?
Quelle est cette gare?
Kel ay set gar?

How long does the train stop here?
Combien de temps le train s'arrête-t-il ici?
Combya(n) de(r) tah(n) le(r) tra(n) sarret-teel eessee?

What time do we get to Paris/ the frontier?
A quelle heure arrive-t-on à Paris/ la frontière?
A kel er arreev-toh(n) a Paree/ la froh(n)tyair?

Is this Clermont-Ferrand?

Est-ce bien Clermont-Ferrand?
Ess bya(n) Clairmoh(n)-
  Ferrah(n)?

Are there any couchettes free?

Y a-t-il des couchettes libres?
Yateel day coushet leebr?

Would you wake me at 6 o'clock?

**Voudriez-vous me réveiller à six
  heures du matin?**
Voodryay-voo me(r) rayvayay a
  seezer dew matah(n)?

Is there a first-aid box on the
  train?

**Y a-t-il une trousse de premiers
  soins dans le train?**
Yateel ewn trooss de(r) premyay
  swa(n) dah(n) le(r) tra(n)?

Arrivals

What time does the Toulouse train
  get in?

**A quelle heure arrive le train de
  Toulouse?**
A kel er arreev le(r) tra(n) de(r)
  Toolooz?

What platform does it come in at?

Sur quelle voie arrive-t-il?
Sewr kel vwa arreev-teel?

Is it late?

Est-il en retard?
Eteel ah(n) retar?

*No, it's on time.

Non, il est à l'heure.
Noh(n), eel ay taller.

*It is running twenty minutes late.

Il a un retard de vingt minutes.
Eel a uh(n) retar de(r) vah(n)
  meenewt.

Porters and baggage

Where do I pick up my registered
  luggage?

**Où dois-je reprendre mes bagages
  enregistrés?**
Oo dwazh reprah(n)dr may
  bagahzh ah(n)rezheestray?

That's not my luggage.	**Ces bagages-là ne sont pas à moi.**
	Say bagahzh-la ne(r) soh(n) pah a mwa.
How much is it per case?	**C'est combien par valise?**
	Say combya(n) par valeez?
How much do I owe you?	**Combien vous dois-je?**
	Combya(n) voo dwazh?
I can't find the porter with my baggage.	**Je n'arrive pas à trouver le porteur qui a mes valises.**
	Zhe(r) narreev pah a troovay le(r) porter kee a may valeez.

Difficulties

I have lost my ticket.	**J'ai perdu mon billet.**
	Zhay pairdew moh(n) beeyay.
I have left my luggage on the train.	**J'ai laissé mes bagages dans le train.**
	Zhay laysay may bagahzh dah(n) le(r) tra(n).
I have missed the train. Is there a later one?	**J'ai manqué le train. Est-ce qu'il y en a un autre plus tard?**
	Zhay mah(n)kay le(r) tra(n). Esskeelyona uhnohtr plew tar?
I got on the wrong train by mistake.	**Je me suis trompé de train.**
	Zhe(r) me(r) swee troh(n)pay de(r) tra(n).
I'll pay the excess fare.	**Je paierai le supplément.**
	Zhe payray le(r) sewpplaymah(n).

NOTICES

Accès aux quais	Access to platforms
Défense de fumer	No smoking
Eau non potable	Not drinking water

Grandes Lignes	Main lines
Lignes de Banlieue	Suburban lines
Ne pas se pencher en-dehors	Do not lean out
Réservé aux mutilés de guerre	Reserved for disabled soldiers

Travelling by underground (metro)

Where is the nearest metro station?
Où est la station de métro la plus proche?
Oo ay la stassyoh(n) de(r) maytroh la plew prosh?

Two tickets, please.
Deux tickets, s'il vous plaît.
De(r) teekay, seelvooplay.

A book of tickets, please.
Un carnet de tickets, s'il vous plaît.
Uh(n) carnay de(r) teekay, seelvooplay.

Is this the right direction for . . .?
Est-ce bien la direction de . . .?
Ess bya(n) la deerekssyoh(n) de(r) . . .?

*No, you are going the wrong way.
Non, vous allez dans le sens inverse.
Noh(n), voozallay dah(n) le(r) sah(n)za(n)vairss.

*You should be on the opposite platform.
Vous devriez être sur le quai en face.
Voo de(r)vryayzetr sewr le(r) kay ah(n) fass.

I want to get to . . . Do I have to change?
Je veux me rendre à . . . Dois-je changer?
Zhe(r) ve(r) me(r) rah(n)dr a . . . Dwazh shah(n)zhay?

*Yes, change at . . . .
Oui, changez à . . . .
Wee, shah(n)zhay a . . . .

Travelling by taxi

There is often a set fare between stations, or from station to airport, and you are advised to ask first what the fare is likely to be. After 11.00 p.m. there is a supplementary charge.

Porter, call me a taxi.	**Porteur, appelez-moi un taxi.**
	Porter, applay-mwa uh(n) taxi.
Where is the taxi rank?	**Où est la station de taxis?**
	Oo ay la stassyoh(n) de(r) taxi?
How far is it to . . . ?	**A quelle distance se trouve . . . ?**
	A kel deestah(n)ss se(r) troov . . . ?
Please take me to this address.	**Conduisez-moi à cette adresse, s'il vous plaît.**
	Coh(n)dweezay-mwa a set address seelvooplay.
I'm in a hurry.	**Je suis pressé.**
	Zhe(r) swee pressay.
I would like to book a taxi to the station for 7.00 a.m. tomorrow.	**Je voudrais commander un taxi pour demain matin à sept heures pour aller à la gare.**
	Zhe(r) voodray commah(n)day uh(n) taxi poor dema(n) mata(n) a seter poor allay a la gar.
How much do I owe you?	**Combien vous dois-je?**
	Combya(n) voo dwazh?
Please wait for me. I shall be five minutes.	**Attendez-moi, s'il vous plaît. Je serai cinq minutes.**
	Attah(n)day-mwa seelvooplay. Zhe(r) seray sank meenewt.

Hiring a car

I would like to hire a car/ and driver/for the day.	**Je voudrais louer une voiture/avec chauffeur/pour la journée.**
	Zhe(r) voodray looay ewn vwatewr/avec shohfer/poor la zhoornay.
How much does it cost ...	**Quel est le prix ...**
	Kel ay le(r) pree ...
– for an hour?	**– à l'heure?**
	– a ler?
– for a day?	**– par jour?**
	– par zhoor?
– for a weekend?	**– pour un weekend?**
	– poor uh(n) weekend?
– for a week?	**– par semaine?**
	– par smen?
Do you have any small/large cars for hire?	**Avez-vous/de petites/de grandes/ voitures à louer?**
	Avay-voo/de(r) pe(r)teet/de(r) grah(n)d/vwatewr a looay?
Have you any English make cars?	**Avez-vous des voitures à fabrication anglaise?**
	Avay-voo day vwatewr a fabreekassyoh(n) ah(n)glez?

Travelling by plane

Procedure at airports is international, and if you get into any difficulties you are sure to find someone who speaks English.

The address of Air France in London is:

> 158 New Bond Street,
> London W1.

For internal flights in France, contact:

Air Inter,
232 rue de Rivoli,
Paris 75001.

Travelling by bus or coach

French buses are single-deckers and usually have more standing than sitting space. In most buses you pay as you enter, and in large towns you can buy a book of tickets if you intend to make several journeys.

French people are not in the habit of forming queues at bus stops and all rush for the door at once when the bus arrives, so be prepared to use your elbows.

Where is the bus (coach) station?	Où est la gare routière?
	Oo ay la gar rootyair?
Where is the bus stop?	Où est l'arrêt d'autobus?
	Oo ay larray dohtohbooss?
Where does the bus to . . . leave from?	Où dois-je prendre l'autobus pour . . .?
	Oo dwazh prah(n)dr lohtohbooss poor . . .?
Do I need to book a seat?	Faut-il réserver une place?
	Foh-teel rayzairvay ewn plass?
What time does the first/last/next bus leave?	A quelle heure part le premier/dernier/prochain autobus?
	A kel er par le(r) premyay/dairnyay/prosha(n) ohtohbooss?
Does this bus go to the station?	Cet autobus va-t-il à la gare?
	Set ohtohbooss vateel a la gar?

*No, you should take a no. 12.

Non, il vous faut le douze.
Noh(n), eel voo foh le(r) dooze.

Which bus goes to the beach?

Quel est l'autobus pour la plage?
Kel ay lohtohbooss poor la plazh?

*You need a no. 3 bus for the beach.

Vous devez prendre le bus numéro trois pour la plage.
Voo de(r)vay prah(n)dr le(r) booss newmairoh trwa poor la plazh.

How often do the buses leave for the city centre?

Quelle est la fréquence des autobus pour le centre de la ville?
Kel ay la fraykah(n)ss daze ohtohbooss poor le(r) sah(n)tr de(r) la veel.

*They leave every 15 minutes/ twice a day.

Ils partent/toutes les quinze minutes/deux fois par jour.
Eel part/toot lay kah(n)z meenyout/de(r) fwa par zhoor.

Is this the bus from Cherbourg, please?

Est-ce bien l'autobus de Cherbourg, s'il vous plaît?
Ess bya(n) lohtohbooss de(r) Shairboor, seelvooplay?

Is this the right direction for . . . ?

Est-ce bien la direction de . . . ?
Ess bya(n) la deerekssyoh(n) de(r) . . . ?

*No, you should be on the other side of the road.

Non, vous devriez être de l'autre côté de la rue.
Noh(n), voo devryay etr de(r) lohtr cohtay de(r) la rew.

Please can you tell me when to get off?

Pouvez-vous me dire quand je dois descendre, s'il vous plaît?
Poovay-voo me(r) deer ka(n) zhe(r) dwa dessah(n)dr, seelvooplay?

Is there an excursion to Mont Saint-Michel?

Y a-t-il une excursion au Mont Saint-Michel?
Yateel ewn exkoorssoyh(n) oh Moh(n) Sah(n)-Meeshel?

Which is the coach to Paris?

Quel est le car pour Paris?
Kel ay le(r) car poor Paree?

*It's that one.

C'est celui-là.
Say selwee-la.

*It's over there.

C'est là-bas.
Say la-bah.

*It hasn't come yet.

Il n'est pas encore arrivé.
Eel nay paahzah(n)kor arreevay.

*It's just left.

Il vient de partir.
Eel vya(n) de(r) parteer.

At the Hotel

If you have not booked at a particular hotel it is a good idea to take with you a hotel list such as that issued by Michelin or by one of the British motoring organisations. Also useful is the Logis de France leaflet, which is obtainable from the French Government Tourist Office in London. As well as these publications you will find that each town **Syndicat d'Initiative** (see p. 107) issues its own local list of recommended hotels. This is always worth consulting and the traveller can see exactly what to expect as regards price. There are five categories of hotel in France.

It is worth noting that you always pay for the room, not for the number of people in it. The price of a double room is less than twice the price of a single room. The price should be displayed on the back of the bedroom door, and the cost of breakfast, service charge and taxes should also be shown. You usually have the choice of full board **(pension complète)**, which includes breakfast, lunch and dinner, half board **(demi-pension)**, which includes breakfast and one other meal, or simply bed and breakfast. Most hotels have their own bar and the larger ones have a restaurant.

Every visitor staying overnight in France is required to register with the police. This is usually done for you if you are staying at a hotel by the hotelier, who will ask you to fill in a form **(fiche)** on arrival at the hotel. You sometimes have to surrender your passport for this purpose, but it is usually returned to you promptly.

Booking a room

I have booked a room.

J'ai réservé une chambre.
Zhay rayzairvay ewn shah(n)br.

I would like to book a room for one night.	Je voudrais une chambre pour une nuit.
	Zhe(r) voodray ewn shah(n)br poor ewn nwee.
My name is	Je m'appelle ....
	Zhe(r) mappell ....
*Have you reserved a room?	Avez-vous réservé une chambre?
	Avay-voo raysairvay ewn shah(n)br?
I wrote to you four weeks ago.	Je vous ai écrit il y a quatres semaines.
	Zhe(r) voozay aicree eelya katr semayn.
Didn't you get my letter?	N'avez-vous pas reçu ma lettre?
	Navay-voo pah resew ma letr?
*I'm sorry but the hotel is full.	Je regrette, mais l'hôtel est complet.
	Zhe(r) regrett, may lohtel ay complay.
I want to stay one night/three nights/one week.	Je voudrais rester une nuit/trois nuits/une semaine.
	Zhe(r) voodray restay ewn nwee/trwa nwee/ewn semayn.
I want a room with shower/with bath.	Je voudrais une chambre avec douche/avec salle de bain.
	Zhe(r) voodray ewn shah(n)br avec doosh/avec sall de(r) ba(n).
I would like a double room/a single room.	Je voudrais une chambre pour deux personnes/pour une personne.
	Zhe(r) voodray ewn shah(n)br poor de(r) pairson/poor ewn pairson.
Have you a room with a balcony?	Avez-vous une chambre avec balcon?
	Avay-voo ewn shah(n)br avec balcoh(n)?

Can we see the room, please?	**Peut-on voir la chambre, s'il vous plaît?**
	Pe(r)toh(n) vwahr la shah(n)br, seelvooplay?
I do not like this room.	**Je n'aime pas cette chambre.**
	Zhe(r) naym pah set shah(n)br.
This room is too large/too small.	**Cette chambre est trop grande/trop petite.**
	Set shah(n)br ay troh grah(n)d/troh pe(r)teet.
Have you another room?	**Avez-vous une autre chambre?**
	Avay-vooz ewn ohtr shah(n)br?
Have you a cheaper room?	**Avez-vous une chambre à meilleur marché?**
	Avay-vooz ewn shah(n)br a mayer marshay?
*I'm sorry, this is the only room available.	**Je regrette, mais c'est la seule chambre libre.**
	Zhe(r) regrett, may say la serl shah(n)br leebr.
*We shall have another room free tomorrow.	**Nous aurons une autre chambre libre demain.**
	Noozoroh(n) ewn ohtr shah(n)br leebr dema(n).
We'd like a room with twin beds.	**Nous désirons une chambre à lits jumeaux.**
	Noo dayzeeroh(n) zewn shah(n)br a lee zhewmoh.
Have you a room which faces the sea?	**Avez-vous une chambre qui donne sur la mer?**
	Avay-vooz ewn shah(n)br kee don soor la mair?
Is the room quiet?	**La chambre est tranquille?**
	La shah(n)br ay trah(n)kee?
I like this room.	**J'aime cette chambre.**
	Zhaym set shah(n)br.

How much is this room?	**Quel est le prix de cette chambre?**
	Kel ay le(r) pree de(r) set shah(n)br?
How much does it cost without meals?	**Quel est le prix sans repas?**
	Kel ay le(r) pree sah(n) re(r)pah?
How much is it for full board/ half board?	**Quel est le prix avec pension complète/demi pension?**
	Kel ay le(r) pree avec pah(n)ssyoh(n) complett/ de(r)mee-pah(n)ssyoh(n)?
How much for bed and breakfast?	**Quel est le prix de la chambre avec petit déjeuner?**
	Kel ay le(r) pree de(r) la shah(n)br avec pe(r)tee dayzhernay?
Is there a reduction for children?	**Y a-t-il un tarif réduit pour les enfants?**
	Yateel uh(n) tareef raydwee poor lez ah(n)fah(n)?
Have you a weekly rate?	**Avez-vous un tarif hebdomadaire?**
	Avay-voo zuh(n) tareef ebdomadair?
Yes, I shall take this room.	**Oui, je prends cette chambre.**
	Wee, zhe(r) prah(n) set shah(n)br.

At the reception

*Please fill in the form.	**Voulez-vous remplir la fiche, s'il vous plaît?**
	Voolay-voo rah(n)pleer la feesh, seelvooplay?
When can I have my passport back?	**Quand me rendrez-vous le passeport?**
	Kah(n) me rah(n)dray-voo le passpor?

Is there a garage/car park?	**Y a-t-il un garage/un parking?** Yateel uh(n) garahzh/uh(n) parkeeng?
What time does the hotel close?	**A quelle heure fermez-vous le soir?** A kel er fairmay-voo le(r) swahr?
*Your room is number 7, on the first floor.	**Votre chambre est le numéro sept, au premier étage.** Votr shah(n)br ay le(r) numeroh set, oh pre(r)myay aytazh.
*The porter will bring up your luggage.	**Le chasseur fera monter vos bagages.** Le(r) shasser fe(r)ra montay voh bagazh.
Please bring up my luggage.	**Faites monter les bagages, s'il vous plaît.** Fayt montay lay bagazh, seelvooplay.
My key, please.	**Ma clef, s'il vous plaît.** Ma klay, seelvooplay.
I have lost my key.	**J'ai perdu ma clef.** Zhay pairdew ma klay.
What time is breakfast served?	**A quelle heure sert-on le petit déjeuner?** A kel er sairtoh(n) le(r) pe(r)tee dayzhernay?
Where is the restaurant?	**Où se trouve le restaurant?** Oo se(r) troov le(r) restorah(n)?
Are there any letters for me?	**Y a-t-il du courrier pour moi?** Yateel dew cooryay poor mwa?
I want to see the manager.	**Je voudrais voir le gérant.** Zhe(r) voodray vwahr le(r) zhayrah(n).
I have lost	**J'ai perdu ....** Zhay pairdew ....
Someone has stolen it.	**Quelqu'un me l'a volé.** Kelkuh(n) me(r) la vollay.

I want to make a phone-call.

Je voudrais téléphoner.
Zhe voodray telefonnay.

About the room

Where are the pillows?

Où sont les oreillers?
Oo soh(n) lezorayay?

The bell/the radio doesn't work.

**La sonnette/la radio ne marche
pas.**
La sonnett/la rahdeeoh ne(r)
marsh pah.

There is no hot water in the tap.

Il n'y a pas d'eau chaude.
Eelnyapah doh shohd.

There are no towels.

Il n'y a pas de serviettes.
Eelnyapah de(r) sairvyet.

The basin doesn't have a plug.

Le lavabo n'a pas de bouchon.
Le(r) lavaboh napah de(r)
booshoh(n).

I should like an extra blanket.

**Je voudrais une couverture
supplémentaire.**
Zhe voodray ewn coovairtewr
sewplaymah(n)tair.

Please bring me a bottle of mineral
water.

**Apportez-moi de l'eau minérale,
s'il vous plaît.**
Aportay-mwa de(r) loh minerahl,
seelvooplay.

Is the central heating working?

**Est-ce que le chauffage central
marche?**
Esske(r) le(r) shohfahzh
sah(n)trahl marsh?

It is cold/hot in here.

Il fait froid/chaud ici.
Eel fay frwah/shoh eessee.

Can you turn the heating down?

Pouvez-vous baisser le chauffage?
Poovay-voo bayssay le(r)
shohfahzh?

Does the window open?	**Peut-on ouvrir la fenêtre?** Pertoh(n) oovreer la fe(r)netr?
The light-bulb is broken.	**L'ampoule est cassée.** Lah(n)pool ay cassay.

Checking out

Please prepare my bill.	**Voulez-vous me préparer la note, s'il vous plaît?** Voolay-voo me(r) prepahray la nott, seelvooplay?
I have to leave early tomorrow morning.	**Je dois partir demain matin de bonne heure.** Zhe(r) dwa parteer de(r)ma(n) mata(n) de(r) bonn er.
Please wake me at seven.	**Réveillez-moi à sept heures.** Rayvayay-mwa a set er.
Please bring down my luggage.	**Faites descendre mes bagages, s'il vous plaît.** Fayt daysah(n)dr may bagahzh, seelvooplay.
Could you change a traveller's cheque?	**Pouvez-vous encaisser un chèque de voyage?** Poovay-voo ah(n)cayssay uh(n) shek de(r) vwa-yahzh?

VOCABULARY

twin beds	**les lits jumeaux**	lay lee zhewmoh
double bed	**le grand lit**	le(r) grah(n) lee
single bed	**le lit pour une personne**	le(r) lee poor ewn pairsson
coat-hanger	**le cintre**	le(r) sa(n)tr
dining-room	**la salle à manger**	la sall a mah(n)zhay

first floor	**le premier étage**	le(r) pre(r)myay aytahzh
second floor	**le deuxième étage**	le(r) derzyem aytahzh
ground floor	**le rez-de-chaussée**	le(r) rayde(r)shohssay
garage	**le garage**	le(r) garahzh
lavatory	**les WC, les toilettes**	lay dooblvaysay, lay twalett
lift	**l'ascenseur**	lassah(n)sser
light	**la lampe électrique**	la lah(n)p electreek
mattress	**le matelas**	le(r) matlah
sheet	**le drap**	le(r) drah
shower	**la douche**	la doosh
shutter	**le volet**	le(r) vollay
suitcase	**la valise**	la valeez
switch	**l'interrupteur**	la(n)tairupter
tap	**le robinet**	le(r) robeenay
towel	**la serviette**	la sairvyet

Information on youth-hostelling in France and the International Youth Hostel handbook are available from:

The YHA,
29 John Adam Street,
London WC2N 6JE.

The equivalent address in France is:

Fédération Unie des Auberges de Jeunesse,
56 rue Blanche,
Paris 75009.

As a general rule, you need to be aged between six and thirty (children under fourteen should be accompanied by an adult or group leader) and to possess a valid International Youth Hostel membership card in order to stay at a youth hostel in France. Fees vary according to category. The hostel regulations, which again vary from hostel to hostel, should be observed. If you are thinking of staying at a French youth hostel during the busy months of July and August, you are well advised to book beforehand. The maximum length of stay at some hostels is three consecutive nights, though others will allow you to stay up to a week, depending on the time of year.

Is there a youth hostel in this town?	Est-ce qu'il y a une auberge de jeunesse dans cette ville? Esskeelya ewn ohbairzh de(r) zhe(r)ness dah(n) set veel?
Is there a youth hostel near here?	Y a-t-il une AJ près d'ici? Yateel ewn Ah-Zhee pray deessee?

Where is it?

Où se trouve-t-il?
Oo se(r) troov-teel?

What time does the hostel open?

A quelle heure ouvre l'auberge?
A kel er oovr lohbairzh?

I want to stay here for one night/
two nights/a week.

**Je veux rester ici une nuit/deux
nuits/une semaine.**
Zhe(r) ve(r) resstay eessee ewn
nwee/de(r) nwee/ewn smen.

What is the fee for the night?

Quel est le prix d'hébergement?
Kel ay le(r) pree
daybairzhmah(n)?

*I am afraid the hostel is full.

**Je regrette, l'auberge est
complète.**
Zhe(r) regret, lohbairzh ay
co(n)plet.

I have lost my membership card.

J'ai perdu ma carte d'hébergement.
Zhay pairdew ma cart
daybairzhmah(n).

Here is my international
youth-hostelling card.

**Voici ma carte internationale
d'AJ.**
Vwassee ma cart
ah(n)tairnassyohnal dAh-Zhee.

*You can only stay for three
nights.

**Vous pouvez rester trois nuits
seulement.**
Voo poovay restay trwa nwee
se(r)lemah(n).

Can I join here?

Puis-je m'inscrire ici?
Pweezh mah(n)skreer eessee?

I wrote to you from England.

Je vous ai écrit d'Angleterre.
Zhe(r) voozay aykree
dAh(n)gletair.

I reserved a place for three nights
at this hostel.

**J'ai réservé une place pour trois
nuits à cette auberge.**
Zhay rayzairvay ewn plass poor
trwa nwee a set ohbairzh.

My name is . . . .

Je m'appelle . . . .
Zhe(r) mappell . . . .

Can we stay in the hostel during the day?

Peut-on rester à l'auberge pendant la journée?
Pe(r)toh(n) restay a lohbairzh pah(n)dah(n) la zhoornay?

What time do we have to be out in the morning?

A quelle heure doit-on partir le matin?
A kel er dwatoh(n) parteer le(r) mata(n)?

What time do we have to be in at night?

A quelle heure doit-on rentrer le soir?
A kel er dwatoh(n) rah(n)tray le(r) swahr?

Can you recommend a good, cheap hotel?

Pouvez-vous recommander un bon hôtel, pas trop cher?
Poovay-voo recommah(n)day uh(n) boh(n) ohtel, pah troh shair?

Can I camp in the hostel grounds?

Est-ce que le camping est autorisé sur le terrain d'AJ?
Esske(r) le(r) cah(n)peeng aytohtohreezay sewr le(r) terra(n) dAh-Zhee?

Where can we leave our bicycles/provisions/rucksacks?

Où pouvons-nous laisser nos bicyclettes/provisions/sacs à dos?
Oo poovoh(n)noo layssay noh beesseeklet/proveezyoh(n)/sak a doh?

Where can I leave my car?

Où puis-je laisser ma voiture?
Oo pweezh layssay ma vwatewr?

Can one have meals at the hostel?

Peut-on prendre les repas à l'auberge?
Pe(r)toh(n) prah(n)dr lay repah a lohbairzh?

How much do they cost? **Combien coûtent-ils?**
Combya(n) coot-teel?

Can I do my own cooking in the kitchen? **Puis-je préparer mes propres repas dans la cuisine?**
Pweezh prayparay may propr repah dah(n) la kweezeen?

What is the charge for use of the kitchen? **Combien demandez-vous pour l'utilisation de la cuisine?**
Combya(n) demah(n)day-voo poor lewteeleezassyoh(n) de(r) la kweezeen?

Where can I buy food? **Où puis-je acheter de la nourriture?**
Oo pweezh ashtay de(r) la noorreetewr?

Do you have packed meals? **Avez-vous des plats à emporter?**
Avay-voo day plah a ah(n)portay?

Can I hire a sleeping bag? **Puis-je louer un sac de couchage?**
Pweezh looay uh(n) sac de(r) cooshahzh?

*Do you have a sheet sleeping bag? **Avez-vous un sac intérieur?**
Avay-voo uh(n) sac ah(n)tairyer?

Have you any more blankets? **Avez-vous des couvertures supplémentaires?**
Avay-voo day coovairtyour sewplaymah(n)tair?

I would like a pillow. **Il me faut un oreiller.**
Eel me(r) foh-tuhnorayay.

Where are the baths/showers/ wash basins? **Où sont les bains/lavabos/ douches?**
Oo soh(n) lay ba(n)/lavaboh/ doosh?

Where is the communal sitting-room? **Où est la salle commune?**
Oo ay la sal commewn?

Is there any hot water? **Y a-t-il de l'eau chaude?**
Yateel de(r) loh shohd?

Camping and Caravanning

Camping is very highly organised on the continent, and is becoming a more popular and sophisticated pastime every year. Sites are graded into categories of one to four stars. Charges for the higher categories can be quite steep, but the lower-graded sites are often just as pleasant, though with fewer facilities.

Some camp sites are open all year round, others from Easter (or May) to the end of September or October. If you intend to camp in July or August, you should book. At some camps, caravans, tents or chalets can be hired and you should write to the camp for details.

You will be charged per person, vehicle and tent or caravan. Lists showing prices, categories, etc. are obtainable from the French Government Tourist Office, 178 Piccadilly, London W1R 0EN.

Is there a camp site near here?	**Est-ce qu'il y a un terrain de camping près d'ici?**
	Esskeelya uh(n) terra(n) de(r) cah(n)peeng pray deessee?
Is this camp official?	**Est-ce que ce terrain de camping est homologué?**
	Esske(r) se(r) terra(n) de(r) cah(n)peeng ay ohmologay?
Can we camp here?	**Peut-on camper ici?**
	Pe(r)toh(n) cah(n)pay eessee?
I have ...	**J'ai ...**
	Zhay ...
– a car.	– une voiture.
	– ewn vwatewr.
– two tents.	– deux tentes.
	– de(r) tah(n)t.

– a caravan.	– une caravane.
	– ewn caravan.
– a dinghy.	– un canot.
	– uh(n) canoh.
– a trailer.	– une remorque.
	– ewn remork.
What is the tariff?	Quel est le tarif?
	Kel ay le(r) tareef?
How much is it per person/tent?	C'est combien par personne/tente?
	Say combya(n) par pairson/tah(n)t?
We would like to stay for two weeks.	Nous voudrions rester quinze jours.
	Noo voodryoh(n) restay kah(n)z zhoor.
Here is my international camping carnet.	Voici mon carnet international de camping.
	Vwassee moh(n) carnay ah(n)tairnassyoh(n)al de(r) cah(n)peeng.
Where should we put the tents?	Où devons-nous dresser les tentes?
	Oo devoh(n) noo dressay lay tah(n)t?
Show me a shadier place. There is too much sun here.	Montrez-moi un endroit plus ombragé. Il y a trop de soleil ici.
	Moh(n)tray-mwa uhnah(n)drwa plewzoh(n)brazhay. Eelya troh de(r) solay eessee.
What time does the camp shut at night?	A quelle heure est-ce que le camping ferme le soir?
	A kel er esske(r) le(r) cah(n)peeng fairm le(r) swahr?
Is there a shop?	Est-ce qu'il y a un magasin?
	Esskeelya uh(n) magaza(n)?
Is there a bar/restaurant on the camp site?	Y a-t-il un bar/restaurant dans le camping?
	Yateel uh(n) bar/restohrah(n) dah(n) le(r) cah(n)peeng?

Is there a drying-room/launderette on the camp site?	**Y a-t-il un séchoir à linge/une laverie automatique dans le camping?** Yateel uh(n) saishwahr a la(n)zh/ ewn lavaree ohtohmateek dah(n) le(r) cah(n)peeng?
Is this drinking water?	**Est-ce que cette eau est potable?** Esske(r) setoh ay potahbl?

SIGNS AND NOTICES

Défense de laver la vaisselle dans les lavabos	No washing up in the basins
Eau potable	Drinking water
Messieurs les campeurs sont priés de déposer leurs ordures dans les endroits prévus à cet effet	Campers are requested to dispose of their rubbish in the places provided
Parking obligatoire	Compulsory car park
Réservé aux caravanes	Caravans only
Prise électrique pour rasoirs	Electric point for shavers

VOCABULARY

air bed	**le matelas pneumatique** le(r) matelah newmateek
bottle-opener	**l'ouvre-bouteille** loovr-bootay
bucket	**le seau** le(r) soh
calor gas	**le camping gaz** le(r) cah(n) peeng gaz
camp-bed	**le lit de camp** le(r) lee de(r) cah(n)p
camp-chair	**la chaise pliante** la shez pleeah(n)t
corkscrew	**le tire-bouchon** le(r) teer-booshoh(n)
fly-sheet	**la toile extérieure** la twal extairyer
groundsheet	**le tapis de sol** le(r) tapee de(r) sol
guy rope	**le cordon de tente** le(r) cordoh(n) de(r) tah(n)t
insecticide	**l'insecticide** lah(n)sekteesseed

matches	**les allumettes**	laze allewmet
methylated spirits	**l'alcool à bruler**	lalko-ol a brewlay
paraffin	**le pétrole**	le(r) paytrol
paraffin lamp	**la lampe à pétrole**	la lah(n)p a paytrol
pitch	**l'emplacement**	lah(n)plassmah(n)
pump (air)	**la pompe (à air)**	la pomp (a air)
rope	**la corde**	la cord
rucksack	**le sac à dos**	le(r) sak a doh
skewer	**la brochette**	la broshet
sleeping bag	**le sac de couchage**	le(r) sak de(r) cooshahzh
stove	**le poêle**	le(r) pwal
tent peg	**le piquet**	le(r) peekay
tin-opener	**l'ouvre-boîte**	loovrbwat
torch	**la lampe de poche**	la lah(n)p de(r) posh

Restaurants, Cafés and Bars

Breakfast **le petit déjeuner** le(r) pe(r)tee dayzhernay
Lunch **le déjeuner** le(r) dayzhernay
Dinner **le dîner** le(r) deenay

The French breakfast is smaller than the traditional English one and consists usually of coffee or hot chocolate, bread or rolls (often without butter) and jam or honey. Of the two main meals lunch is generally considered to be the more important, particularly in the home. There are many different types and categories of restaurant. Naturally some are very expensive, but it is still possible to get a good and relatively cheap meal if you know where to go. For example, if you are motoring you can strike lucky at a **restaurant des routiers** (French equivalent of our transport café which serves simple but often very good food).

Before going into a restaurant it is worth examining the menu, which is usually displayed in the window. This will give you some idea of what the meal will cost. It is also a good idea to keep a look-out for a **menu du jour** or **menu à prix fixe** (a set meal at a fixed price which often includes a small carafe of wine). In the tourist season you will often see advertised a **menu gastronomique**; this will offer regional specialities and other good dishes but is usually fairly expensive.

There are four main courses: soup or hors d'œuvre; fish or omelette (sometimes omitted); meat (vegetables often served separately); dessert or cheese. Bread is eaten with all courses. Wine is the usual drink, but you can, of course, order beer or fruit-juice if you prefer. A cover charge **(le couvert)** is usually made for every person and VAT (in French TVA) is added to the bill. Service is not included unless the bill is marked specifically **'Service Compris'**. It is usual to leave a tip of 12% to 15%.

Meal-times Lunch is usually served from noon to about 3.00 p.m. and dinner from about 8.00 p.m. onwards. Bars and cafés are open from early in the morning to late at night and often serve breakfast. You can get coffee and alcoholic drinks there.

Booking and ordering

Can you recommend a good restaurant?	**Connaissez-vous un bon restaurant, s'il vous plaît?** Conayssay-voo uh(n) boh(n) restorah(n), seelvooplay?
Not too expensive.	**Pas trop cher.** Pah troh shair.
I have reserved a table.	**J'ai réservé une table.** Zhay raysairvay ewn tabl.
My name is	**Je m'appelle ....** Zhe(r) mappell ....
I want to book a table for four at 7 o'clock.	**Je voudrais réserver une table pour quatre pour sept heures.** Zhe(r) voodray raysairvay ewn tabl poor katr poor set er.
*I'm sorry, we have no tables tonight.	**Je regrette, mais nous n'avons pas de tables libres ce soir.** Zhe(r) regrett, may noo navoh(n) pah de(r) tabl leebr se(r) swahr.
*We don't serve dinner till 8 o'clock.	**Nous ne servons pas le dîner avant huit heures.** Noo ne(r) sairvoh(n) pah le(r) deenay avah(n) wheet er.
Have you a table for four/six?	**Avez-vous une table pour quatre/six personnes?** Avay-vooz ewn tabl poor katr/seess pairson?

*We will have a table free in half an hour.	**Nous aurons une table libre dans une demi-heure.**
	Noo zoroh(n) ewn tabl leebr dah(n)z ewn dc(r)mee-er.
A table for two, please.	**Deux couverts, s'il vous plaît.**
	De(r) coovair, seelvooplay.
We are in a hurry.	**Nous sommes pressés.**
	Noo som pressay.
Have you a set menu?	**Avez-vous un menu à prix fixe?**
	Avay-voo uh(n) me(r)new a pree feex?
May we see the menu/the wine list?	**Pourrions-nous voir le menu/la carte des vins?**
	Pooryoh(n)-noo vwahr le(r) me(r)new/la cart day va(n)?
What is the speciality of the house?	**Quel est la spécialité de la maison?**
	Kel ay la spessyaleetay de(r) la mayzoh(n)?
What do you recommend?	**Qu'est-ce que vous recommendez?**
	Kesske(r) voo re(r)comah(n)day?
What does this mean?	**Qu'est-ce que cela veut dire?**
	Kesske(r) sla ve(r) deer?
Can you tell me what this is?	**Pourriez-vous me dire ce que c'est?**
	Pooryay-voo me(r) deer se(r) ke(r) say?
We will have the menu at 19 francs.	**Nous prenons le menu à dix-neuf francs.**
	Noo pre(r)noh(n) le(r) me(r)new a deess-nerf frah(n).
Is the drink included?	**Boisson comprise?**
	Bwassoh(n) co(n)preez?
*How do you like your steak?	**Comment voulez-vous votre steak?**
	Comah(n) voolay-voo votr stek?
Well done/medium/rare.	**Bien cuit/à point/saignant.**
	Byah(n) cwee/a pwa(n)/ saynjah(n).

A glass of beer, please.	**Une bière, s'il vous plaît.**
	Ewn beer, seelvooplay.
Do you sell wine by the glass?	**Est-ce qu'on sert du vin au verre?**
	Esskoh(n) sair dew va(n) oh vair?
A carafe of local red wine, please.	**Une carafe de vin rouge du pays, s'il vous plaît.**
	Ewn caraff de(r) va(n) roozh dew payee, seelvooplay.
We should like a bottle of white/ red/dry/sweet wine.	**Nous voudrions une bouteille de vin blanc/rouge/sec/doux.**
	Noo voodryoh(n) ewn bootay de(r) va(n) blah(n)/roozh/sec/ doo.
Some water, please.	**De l'eau, s'il vous plaît.**
	De(r) loh, seelvooplay.
Could we have some more . . . ?	**Peut-on avoir encore de . . . ?**
	Pertoh(n) avwahr ah(n)cor de(r) . . . ?
I'd like , . . .	**Je voudrais . . . .**
	Zhe(r) voodray . . . .
Some coffee, please.	**Du café, s'il vous plaît.**
	Dew cafay, seelvooplay.
An ashtray, please.	**Un cendrier, s'il vous plaît.**
	Uh(n) sah(n)dreeay, seelvooplay.
Where is the toilet?	**Où sont les toilettes?**
	Oo soh(n) lay twalet?
Waiter!	**Garçon!**
	Garssoh(n)!
Waitress!	**Mademoiselle!**
	Mamwazel!

Problems

This isn't what I ordered.	**Ce n'est pas ce que j'ai commandé.**
	Se(r) nay pah se(r) ke(r) zhay comah(n)day.

I ordered a	**J'ai commandé . . . .** Zhay comah(n)day . . . .
The soup is cold.	**Le potage est froid.** Le(r) potahzh ay frwa.

The meat/fish is bad.	**La viande/le poisson n'est pas
	  bonne/bon.**
	La vyah(n)d/le(r) pwassoh(n)
	  nay pah bonn/boh(n).

The wine is corked.	**Ce vin sent le bouchon.** Se(r) va(n) sah(n) le(r) booshoh(n).
This is not cooked.	**Ce n'est pas cuit.** Se(r) nay pah cwee.
I should like to see the head waiter.	**Je voudrais voir le maître d'hôtel.** Zhe(r) voodray vwahr le(r) maytr dohtel.
*We have run out of	**Il n'y a plus de . . . .** Eel nya plew de(r) . . . .

Paying the bill

May we have the bill, please.	**L'addition, s'il vous plaît.** Ladeessyoh(n), seelvooplay.
Is service included?	**Le service est compris?** Le(r) sairveess ay co(n)pree?
I think there is a mistake here.	**Je crois qu'il y a une erreur.** Zhe crwa keelya ewn errer.

Thank you, the meal was very
  good
	**Je vous remercie, le repas était
	  très bon.**
	Zhe voo re(r)mairssee, le(r)
	  re(r)pah aytay tray boh(n).

VOCABULARY (for items of food, see 'Food shopping' on p. 67)

ashtray	**le cendrier**	le(r) sah(n)dryay
cover charge	**le couvert**	le(r) coovair
cup	**la tasse**	la tass

fork	**la fourchette** la foorshet
fried	**frit** free
glass	**le verre** le(r) vair
grilled	**grillé** greeay
knife	**le couteau** le(r) cootoh
mustard	**la moutarde** la mootard
napkin	**la serviette** la sairvyet
pepper	**le poivre** le(r) pwavr
plate	**l'assiette** lassyet
poached	**poché** poshay
roasted	**rôti** rohtee
salad	**la salade** la salahd
– green	**la salade verte** la salahd vairt
– mixed	**la salade panachée** la salahd panashay
– fruit	**la macédoine de fruits** la massaydwahn de(r) frwee
salad-dressing	**la vinaigrette** la vinaygret
salt	**le sel** le(r) sel
sauce	**la sauce** la sohss
spoon	**la cuiller** la cweeyay
sweet	**l'entremets** lah(n)trmay
vegetable	**le légume** le(r) laygewm

The above list contains most of the words you are likely to want to *use* in a restaurant. Below is a list of some of the more common dishes you might find on the menu, with approximate English translations:

Les hors d'œuvres (starters)

les crudités	raw salad vegetables
l'artichaut à la vinaigrette	artichoke with oil and vinegar dressing
les tomates farcies	stuffed tomatoes
le melon glacé	iced melon
les escargots	snails

la salade Niçoise	salad with olives, anchovies, tuna fish, etc.
la salade de tomates	tomato salad
le pâté de foie	liver pâté
le pâté de campagne	home-made pâté
les moules marinières	mussels in white-wine sauce
les hors d'œuvres variés	choice of salami and cold meats

Les' ooo

Les œufs (egg dishes)

l'œuf à la coque	boiled egg
l'œuf dur	hard-boiled egg
l'œuf mollet	soft-boiled egg
les œufs brouillés BROOYEAH	scrambled egg
l'œuf sur le plat	fried egg
l'œuf poché	poached egg
l'omelette nature	plain omelette
l'omelette aux fines herbes	omelette with mixed herbs
l'omelette aux tomates	tomato omelette
la mayonnaise	egg mayonnaise
le quiche Lorraine	egg and cheese pie (sometimes with bacon)

TOURNESS — TURNED OVER EASY

Les soupes (soups)

le potage Parmentier	potato soup
le potage Saint-Germain	pea soup
le potage Crécy	carrot soup
le potage bonne femme	potato, carrot and leek soup
le potage aux champignons	mushroom soup
le potage aux cèpes	dried mushroom soup
le potage de lentilles	lentil soup
le pot-au-feu	beef broth
le consommé de gibier	game soup
la soupe à l'oignon	onion soup
la crème vichyssoise glacée	iced potato and leek soup
la soupe de poissons	fish soup

la soupe aux moules	mussel soup with shallots and garlic
le bisque d'homard	lobster chowder

Les poissons (*fish dishes*)

la coquille Saint-Jacques	scallop
les blanchailles frites	fried whitebait
la bouillabaisse	fish stew
les tranches de cabillaud	cod steaks
la darne de saumon grillée	grilled salmon steak
le filet de sole frit	fried fillet of sole
le maquereau grillé	grilled mackerel
la morue à la provençale	salt cod with garlic and onion sauce
les rougets à la meunière	red mullet fried in butter
la mayonnaise de poisson	fish mayonnaise

Les entrées et les rôtis (*meat dishes*)

les côtes de bœuf rôti	roast ribs of beef
le filet de bœuf rôti	roast fillet of beef
le bœuf en daube	braised beef
le bœuf à la bourguignonne	beef stewed with red wine
le ragout de bœuf	brown beef stew
l'estouffade de bœuf	beef stew
le hachis de bœuf	minced beef
le gigot d'agneau	roast leg of lamb
la selle d'agneau	roast saddle of lamb
le navarin d'agneau	brown lamb stew
la blanquette d'agneau	white lamb stew
la côtelette d'agneau	lamb cutlet
la noisette d'agneau	lamb cutlet from the fillet
le carré d'agneau	loin of lamb
le ris d'agneau braisé	braised lamb sweetbreads
la longe de veau	loin of veal
le ris de veau	veal sweetbreads

les médaillons de veau	miniature veal steaks
les escalopes de veau	escalopes of veal
la côte de veau	veal chop
la cervelle au beurre noir	calf's brains in black butter
le cuissot de porc rôti	roast leg of pork
la côte de porc	pork chop
la basse côte de porc rôti	roast spare ribs
le jambon braisé	braised ham
le poulet rôti	roast chicken
le coq au vin	chicken cooked in red wine sauce
le poulet poché au riz	boiled chicken with rice
le poulet au casserole	casserole of chicken
la crêpe de volaille	chicken pancake
le caneton bigarade	duckling with bitter oranges
le canard aux cerises	duck with cherries
le civet de lièvre	jugged hare
les côtelettes de chevreuil	venison cutlets

Shopping

Shops are generally open from Monday to Saturday from 9 a.m. to 6.30 p.m. Some foodshops are open on Sunday morning and most stores are closed on Monday morning. The French use the metric system of weights and measures, and the relevant conversion tables are provided on pp. 80–81. Clothes in general are more expensive than they are in Britain, though there are now numerous supermarkets (**supermarchés**) and even hypermarkets (**hypermarchés**) which sell cheaper clothes as well as a large range of household articles and food.

For ease of reference, this section has been divided into smaller units as follows:

1 Food shopping
2 Clothes and accessories
3 Household and domestic
4 Medicines and cosmetics
5 Photographic materials
6 Books and stationery
7 Cigarettes, tobacco and stamps

1 Food shopping

Bread Bread is bought at the **Boulangerie**. French bread is very light and tasty, but it tends to go stale rather quickly and is best eaten on the day when it is bought. Cakes and pastries are bought at the **Pâtisserie**, which may also have a tea-room (**salon de thé**) attached. Sometimes you will notice the sign **Boulangerie-Pâtisserie** which indicates that you can buy both bread and cakes. The sign **Boulangerie-Confiserie** means that the baker also sells sweets and chocolates. Ice-creams can often be bought at a **Pâtisserie**.

Meat There are three types of butcher's shop in France: the ordinary butcher's is called the **Boucherie**; there is also a shop called the **Boucherie Chevaline** where you can buy horse and stag meat (easily distinguishable from the **Boucherie** by the horse symbol displayed outside). Thirdly, there is the **Charcuterie** or pork-butcher which sells prepared meats such as ham, tongue, pâté and sausages, as well as various prepared hors d'œuvres.

Fish The fishmonger's shop is the **Poissonnerie**, where you can usually find a good selection of fresh fish and sea-food. Remember that shellfish such as mussels and oysters ought to be tightly closed when bought.

General groceries Go to a shop called an **Epicerie** or **Alimentation Générale**. There you can buy tinned foods (**conserves**), biscuits, cheese and milk, frozen foods, etc.

The market The market (**marché**) is still a great institution and French housewives will nearly always go there for their fresh food on market days. The food tends to be both fresher and cheaper.

Is there a market here today?	**Y a-t-il un marché ici aujourd'hui?** Yateel uh(n) marshay eessee ohzhoordwee?
How much is it per pound/per kilo?	**C'est combien la livre/le kilo?** Say coh(n)byah(n) la leevr/le(r) keelo?
I want a kilo of apples, please.	**Donnez-moi un kilo de pommes, s'il vous plaît.** Donnay-mwa uh(n) keelo de(r) pom, seelvooplay.
I should like half a kilo.	**Je voudrais un demi kilo.** Zhe(r) voodray uh(n) de(r)mee keelo.

Please give me four slices.	**Donnez-moi quatre tranches, s'il vous plaît.**
	Donnay-mwa katr trah(n)sh, seelvooplay.
I want half a litre of milk.	**Je voudrais un demi-litre de lait.**
	Zhe(r) voodray uh(n) de(r)mee leetr de(r) lay.
Are these ripe? Is it ripe?	**Sont-ils mûrs? Est-ce que c'est mûr?**
	Soh(n)t-eel mewr? Esske(r) say mewr?
Is it fresh?	**Est-ce que c'est frais?**
	Esske(r) say fray?
Where are the tinned foods, please?	**Où sont les conserves, s'il vous plaît?**
	Oo soh(n) lay coh(n)sairv, seelvooplay?
Have you a smaller tin?	**Avez-vous une boîte plus petite?**
	Avay-vooz ewn bwaht plew pe(r)teet?
Have you a larger packet?	**Avez-vous un paquet plus grand?**
	Avay-vooz uh(n) packay plew grah(n)?
Do you have a carrier-bag?	**Avez-vous un grand sac en papier, s'il vous plaît?**
	Avay-vooz uh(n) grah(n) sac ah(n) papyay, seelvooplay?
I want enough for two/four people.	**J'en voudrais pour deux/quatre personnes.**
	Zhah(n) voodray poor de(r)/katr pairsonn.

VOCABULARY

Meat

beef	le bœuf	le(r) berf

chicken	**le poulet** le(r) poolay
(baby)	**le poussin** le(r) poossa(n)
chop	**la côtelette** la cohtlett
duckling	**le caneton** le(r) cantoh(n)
game	**le gibier** le(r) zheebyay
ham	**le jambon** le zhah(n)boh(n)
hare	**le lièvre** le(r) leeayvre
kidneys	**les rognons** lay rohnjoh(n)
lamb	**l'agneau** lanjoh
liver	**le foie** le(r) fwa
mince	**le hâchis** le(r) ashee
pâté (game)	**le pâté de gibier** le(r) pattay de(r) zheebyay
(liver)	**le pâté de foie** le(r) pattay de(r) fwa
(local)	**le pâté de campagne** le pattay de(r) cah(n)panj
pheasant	**le faisan** le(r) faysah(n)
poultry	**la volaille** la vol-eye
rabbit	**le lapin** le(r) lappa(n)
sausage (small, fresh)	**la saucisse** la sohsseess
(large, dry)	**le saucisson** le(r) sohsseessoh(n)
turkey	**le dindon** le(r) dah(n)doh(n)
veal	**le veau** le voh

Fruit and vegetables

apple	**la pomme** la pom
apricot	**l'abricot** labreecoh
artichoke	**l'artichaut** larteeshoh
asparagus	**les asperges** lez asspairzh
aubergine	**l'aubergine** lohbairzheen
avocado pear	**l'avocat** lavohcah
banana	**la banane** la banann
bean (French)	**le haricot vert** le(r) areecoh vair
(broad)	**la fève** la fayv
(kidney)	**les flageolets** lay flazhayohlay
beetroot	**la betterave** la bettrahv
black-currant	**le cassis** le(r) cassee
blackberry	**la mûre** la mewr
cabbage	**le chou** le(r) shoo

carrot	**la carotte**	la carott
cauliflower	**le chou-fleur**	le(r) shoo-fler
celery (head of)	**(le pied de) céléri**	(le(r) pyay de(r)) saylayree
chicory	**les endives**	lez ah(n)deev
cucumber	**le concombre**	le(r) coh(n)coh(n)mbr
fruit	**le fruit**	le(r) frwee
garlic	**l'ail**	lye
gooseberry	**la groseille**	la grohzaye
grapefruit	**le pamplemousse**	le(r) pah(n)plmooss
grapes	**le raisin**	le(r) rayza(n)
leek	**le poireau**	le(r) pwahroh
lemon	**le citron**	le(r) seetroh(n)
lettuce	**la salade**	la salahd
marrow	**la courge**	la coorzh
melon	**le melon**	le(r) me(r)loh(n)
mushroom	**le champignon**	le(r) shah(n)peenjoh(n)
onion	**l'oignon**	loynjoh(n)
orange	**l'orange**	lorah(n)zh
parsley	**le persil**	le(r) pairsee
parsnip	**le panais**	le(r) pannay
peach	**la pêche**	la pesh
pear	**la poire**	la pwahr
peas	**les petits pois**	lay pe(r)tee pwa
pepper	**le poivre**	le(r) pwahrv
pineapple	**l'ananas**	lananah
plum	**la prune**	la prewn
potato	**la pomme de terre**	la pom de(r) tair
radish	**le radis**	le(r) radee
raspberry	**la framboise**	la frah(n)bwahz
red-currant	**la groseille rouge**	la grohzay roozh
shalot	**l'échalote**	layshallot
spinach	**les épinards**	lez aypeenahr
strawberry	**la fraise**	la frayz
sweetcorn	**le maïs**	le(r) meye-eess
tomato	**la tomate**	la tomaht
turnip	**le navet**	le(r) navay
watercress	**le cresson**	le(r) cressoh(n)

Fish

anchovy	**l'anchoi**	lah(n)shwa
cod	**le cabillaud**	le(r) cabbeeoh
crab	**le crabe**	le(r) crab
crayfish (freshwater)	**l'écrevisse**	laycre(r)veess
(sea)	**la langouste**	la lah(n)goost
eel	**l'anguille**	lah(n)gwee
fish	**le poisson**	le(r) pwassoh(n)
hake	**le colin, la merluche**	le(r) cola(n), la mairlewsh
halibut	**le flétan**	le(r) flaytah(n)
herring	**le hareng**	le(r) arah(n)
lobster	**le homard**	le(r) omahr
mackerel	**le maquereau**	le(r) mackroh
mussels	**les moules**	lay mool
octopus	**le poulpe**	le(r) poolp
oysters	**les huîtres**	lay weetr
prawn	**la crevette**	la cre(r)vett
(Dublin Bay)	**la langoustine**	la lah(n)goosteen
salmon	**le saumon**	le(r) sohmoh(n)
sardine	**la sardine**	la sardeen
shrimp	**la crevette**	la cre(r)vett
skate	**la raie**	la ray
sole	**la sôle**	la sohl
squid	**le calmar**	le(r) calmahr
trout	**la truite**	la trweet
tuna	**le thon**	le(r) toh(n)
turbot	**le turbot**	le(r) turboh
winkle	**le bigorneau**	le(r) beegornoh
whitebait	**la blanchaille**	la blah(n)sh-eye
whiting	**le merlan**	le(r) mairlah(n)

Bread, cakes and sweets

bread	**le pain**	le(r) pa(n)
cake	**le gâteau**	le(r) gattoh
chocolate (eating)	**le chocolat (à croquer)**	le(r) shocohlah (a crockay)

ice-cream	**la glace** la glass	
roll	**le petit pain** le(r) pe(r)tee pa(n)	
(crescent-shaped)	**le croissant** le(r) crwassah(n)	
(sweet)	**la brioche** la breeosh	
tart	**la tarte** la tart	
sweet	**le bonbon** le(r) boh(n)boh(n)	

General groceries

baby food	**les aliments pour enfants** lez alimah(n) poor ah(n)fah(n)	
biscuit	**le biscuit** le(r) beesscwee	
butter	**le beurre** le(r) ber	
cheese	**le fromage** le(r) fromahzh	
coffee (ground)	**le café en poudre** le(r) caffay ah(n) poodr	
(instant)	**le café soluble** le(r) caffay solewbl	
cream	**la crême** la crem	
egg	**l'œuf** le(r)f	
flour	**la farine** la fareen	
honey	**le miel** le(r) myel	
jam	**la confiture** la coh(n)feeture	
margarine	**la margarine** la margareen	
marmalade	**la confiture d'oranges** la coh(n)feetewr dorah(n)zh	
mustard	**la moûtarde** la mootard	
oil (olive)	**l'huile (d'olive)** lweel (doleev)	
pepper	**le poivre** le(r) pwahvr	
rice	**le riz** le(r) ree	
salt	**le sel** le(r) sel	
soup	**la soupe** la soop	
sugar	**le sucre** le sewcr	
tea	**le thé** le(r) tay	
vinegar	**le vinaigre** le(r) vinaygr	
tinned foods	**les conserves** lay coh(n)sairv	

Drinks

apple juice	**le jus de pommes**	le(r) zjew de(r) pom
beer	**la bière**	la byair
cider	**le cidre**	le(r) seedr
fruit juice	**le jus de fruits**	le(r) zhew de(r) frwee
lemonade (fizzy)	**la limonade**	la leemonahd
(still)	**la citronnade**	la seetronahd
orangeade	**l'orangeade**	lorah(n)zhahd
wine	**le vin**	le(r) va(n)

2 Clothes and accessories

I want to buy ....
Je voudrais acheter ....
Zhe(r) voodrayz ashtay ....

I am looking for ....
Je cherche ....
Zhe(r) shairsh ....

I am just looking.
Je regarde seulement.
Zhe(r) re(r)gard serlmah(n).

I want something like this/that.
Je voudrais quelque chose comme ceci/cela.
Zhe(r) voodray kelke(r) shohz com se(r)ssee/se(r)lah.

Something in cotton/terylene.
Quelque chose en coton/en terylène.
Kelke(r) shohz ah(n) cotoh(n)/ah(n) terrylayn.

Have you this in my size?
Avez-vous ceci à ma taille?
Avay-voo se(r)ssee a ma tye?

My size is ....
Ma taille est .... (*See sizes on p.* 80.)
Ma tye ay ....

*I'm sorry, we haven't got it in your size.
Je regrette, mais nous ne l'avons pas dans votre taille.
Zhe(r) re(r)grett, may noo ne(r) laroh(n) pah dah(n) votr tye.

Could you please measure me?	**Voulez-vous prendre mes mesures?** Voolay-voo prah(n)dr may me(r)zewr?
May I try it on?	**Puis-je l'essayer?** Pweezh lessayay?
It doesn't fit me.	**Ça ne me va pas.** Sa ne(r) me(r) va pah.
I don't like it.	**Je ne l'aime pas.** Zhe ne(r) laym pah.
I don't like the colour.	**Je n'aime pas la couleur.** Zhe naym pah la cooler.
Have you a red one?	**En avez-vous en rouge?** Ah(n) avay-voo ah(n) roozh?
It's too big/too small.	**C'est trop grand/trop petit.** Say troh grah(n)/troh pe(r)tee.
It's too long/too short.	**C'est trop long/trop court.** Say troh loh(n)/troh coor.
It's too expensive.	**C'est trop cher.** Say troh shair.
Have you something cheaper?	**Avez-vous quelque chose de meilleur marché?** Avay-voo kelke(r) shohz de(r) mayer marshay?
These shoes are too tight.	**Ces chaussures me serrent trop.** Say shohssewr me(r) sair troh.
These shoes are too loose.	**Ces chaussures sont trop larges.** Say shohssewr soh(n) troh larzh.
The heel is too low/too high.	**Le talon est trop bas/trop haut.** Le(r) talloh(n) ay troh bah/troh oh.
I prefer rubber/leather soles.	**Je préfère la semelle en caoutchouc/en cuir.** Zhe(r) prayfair la se(r)mell ah(n) cowooshoo/ah(n) cweer.
I will take this pair.	**Je prendrai ces chaussures.** Zhe(r) prah(n)dray say shohssewr

How much is it?	**Quel est le prix?**
	Kel ay le(r) pree?
I'll take it.	**Je le prends.**
	Zhe(r) le(r) prah(n).
Do you accept credit cards?	**Acceptez-vous les cartes de crédit?**
	Axeptay-voo lay cart de(r) craydee?
Please may I have a receipt?	**Voulez-vous me donner un reçu, s'il vous plaît?**
	Voolay-voo me(r) donnay uh(n) re(r)sew, seelvooplay?
I would like to change it.	**Je voudrais l'échanger.**
	Zhe(r) voodray layshah(n)zhay.
I bought it two days ago/two weeks ago.	**Je l'ai acheté il y a deux jours/ il y a deux semaines.**
	Zhe(r) lay ashtay eelya de(r) zhoor/eelya de(r) se(r)mayn
Where can I buy . . .?	**Où peut-on acheter . . .?**
	Oo pe(r)toh(n) nashtay . . .?

VOCABULARY

Here are some of the shops you are likely to see:

le grand magasin	department store
le magasin libre-service	self-service store
le magasin de nouveautés	haberdasher's shop
la maroquinerie	leather shop
le magasin de chaussures	shoe shop

And some of the things you might want to buy:

anorak	**l'anorak**	lanorak
bathing costume	**le maillot de bain**	le(r) mayoh de(r) ba(n)
beach robe	**la robe de plage**	la rob de(r) plahzh
belt	**la ceinture**	la sa(n)tewr
bikini	**le bikini**	le(r) beekeeni
blouse	**le corsage**	le(r) corssahzh
boots	**les bottes**	lay bot
bra	**le soutien-gorge**	le(r) sootyah(n)-gorzh
button	**le bouton**	le(r) bootoh(n)
cap	**la casquette**	la casket
cardigan	**le gilet**	le(r) zheelay
coat	**le pardessus**	le(r) parde(r)ssew
dress (evening)	**la robe (de soir)**	la rob (de(r) swahr)
dressing gown	**la robe de chambre**	la rob de(r) shah(n)br
gloves	**les gants**	lay gah(n)
handbag	**le sac à main**	le(r) sac a ma(n)
handkerchief	**le mouchoir**	le(r) mooshwahr
hat	**le chapeau**	le(r) shapoh
heel	**le talon**	le(r) taloh(n)
jacket (ladies')	**la jaquette**	la zhakett
(men's)	**le veston**	le(r) vestoh(n)
jeans	**les blue-jeans**	lay blew-zheen
jersey	**le tricot**	le(r) treecoh
nightdress	**la chemise de nuit**	la she(r)meez de(r) nwee
pants (ladies')	**la culotte**	la cewlot
(men's)	**le slip**	le(r) sleep
petticoat	**le jupon**	le(r) zhewpoh(n)
pullover	**le pullover**	le(r) pewlohvair
pyjamas	**le pyjama**	le(r) peezhamah
raincoat	**l'imperméable**	la(n)pairmayahbl
sandals	**les sandales**	lay sah(n)dahl
scarf	**l'écharpe**	laysharp
(silk)	**le foulard**	le(r) foolahr
shirt	**la chemise**	la she(r)meez
shoes	**les chaussures**	lay shohssewr

shorts	**les shorts**	lay short
slip	**la combinaison**	la coh(n)beenayzoh(n)
slippers	**les chaussettes**	lay shohssett
stockings	**les bas**	lay bah
suit	**le complet**	le(r) coh(n)play
sun-glasses	**les lunettes de soleil**	lay lewnett de(r) solay
sweater	**le chandail**	le(r) shah(n)d-eye
tie	**la cravate**	la cravatt
tights	**les collants**	lay collah(n)
towel	**la serviette**	la sairvyett
T-shirt	**le T-shirt**	le(r) tee-shirt
trousers	**le pantalon**	le(r) pah(n)talloh(n)
vest	**le gilet**	le(r) zheelay
zip-fastener	**la fermeture éclair**	la fairme(r)tewr ayclair

Colours

red	**rouge**	roozh
blue	**bleu**	ble(r)
yellow	**jaune**	zhohn
green	**vert** (*m.*)/**verte** (*f.*)	vair/vairt
white	**blanc** (*m.*)/**blanche** (*f.*)	blah(n)/blah(n)sh
black	**noir**	nwahr
grey	**gris** (*m.*)/**grise** (*f.*)	gree/greez
pink	**rose**	rohz
brown	**brun** (*m.*)/**brune** (*f.*)	bruh(n)/brewn
orange	**orange**	orah(n)zh

Some common materials

cotton	**le coton**	le(r) cottoh(n)
leather	**le cuir**	le(r) cweer
nylon	**le nylon**	le(r) neeloh(n)
plastic	**le plastique**	le(r) plasteek
rubber	**le caoutchouc**	le(r) cowooshoo
silk (printed)	**la soie (imprimée)**	la swa (a(n)preemay)
wool	**la laine**	la layn

terylene	**le térylène**	le(r) tayreelen
suede	**le daim**	le(r) da(n)
crepe	**le crêpe**	le(r) crayp
flannel	**la flannelle**	la flanell
velvet	**le velours**	le(r) ve(r)loor
satin	**le satin**	le(r) satta(n)
poplin	**la popeline**	la popleen
worsted	**la laine peignée**	la layn paynjay

CONVERSION TABLES

This is only a general guide, and it is always advisable to try on clothes etc. before buying them.

Women's clothes

	ENGLISH	FRENCH			ENGLISH	FRENCH
Dresses	32	38	Hats		$6\frac{1}{8}$	50 cm
	34	40			$6\frac{1}{4}$	51
	36	42			$6\frac{3}{8}$	52
	38	44			$6\frac{1}{2}$	53
	40	46			$6\frac{5}{8}$	54
	42	48			$6\frac{3}{4}$	55
					$6\frac{7}{8}$	56
Blouses	30	42			7	57
	32	44			$7\frac{1}{8}$	58
	34	46			$7\frac{1}{4}$	59
	36	48			$7\frac{3}{8}$	60
	38	50			$7\frac{1}{2}$	61
	40	52				
	42	54	Shoes		2	34
					$2\frac{1}{2}$	35
Sweaters	32	42			3	$35\frac{1}{2}$
	34	44			$3\frac{1}{2}$	36
	36	46			4	$36\frac{1}{2}$
	38	48			$4\frac{1}{2}$	$37\frac{1}{2}$
	40	50			5	38
					$5\frac{1}{2}$	$38\frac{1}{2}$
Stockings	8	0			6	39
	$8\frac{1}{2}$	1			$6\frac{1}{2}$	40
	9	2			7	$40\frac{1}{2}$
	$9\frac{1}{2}$	3			$7\frac{1}{2}$	41
	10	4			8	42
	$10\frac{1}{2}$	5				
	11	6				

Men's clothes

	ENGLISH	FRENCH			ENGLISH	FRENCH
Hats	$6\frac{1}{4}$	51		Suits & coats	36	46
	$6\frac{3}{8}$	52			38	48
	$6\frac{1}{2}$	53			40	50
	$6\frac{5}{8}$	54			42	52
	$6\frac{3}{4}$	55			44	54
	$6\frac{7}{8}$	56			46	56
	7	57				
	$7\frac{1}{8}$	58		Shoes	7	$40\frac{1}{2}$
	$7\frac{1}{4}$	59			8	42
	$7\frac{3}{8}$	60			9	43
	$7\frac{1}{2}$	61			10	44
	$7\frac{5}{8}$	62			11	$45\frac{1}{2}$
	$7\frac{3}{4}$	63			12	47
	$7\frac{7}{8}$	64			13	48
Shirts	13	33		Socks	$9\frac{1}{2}$	39
	$13\frac{1}{2}$	34			10	40
	14	35–36			$10\frac{1}{2}$	41
	$14\frac{1}{2}$	37			11	42
	15	38			$11\frac{1}{2}$	43
	$15\frac{1}{2}$	39			12	44
	$15\frac{3}{4}$	40			$12\frac{1}{2}$	45
	16	41				
	$16\frac{1}{2}$	42				
	17	43				

3 Household and domestic

It is necessary to remember that a **Droguerie** is not a chemist, although it sounds like one. At a **droguerie** you can buy some cosmetics and toilet preparations, paints, cleaning materials, etc. The **Quincaillerie** is also a hardware shop, but it approximates more closely to our ironmonger.

I should like a box of	**Je voudrais une boîte de ....** Zhe(r) voodray ewn bwaht de(r) ....
I want a box of matches.	**Je voudrais une boîte d'allumettes.** Zhe(r) voodray ewn bwaht dallewmett.
I should like a bottle of	**Je voudrais une bouteille de ....** Zhe(r) voodray ewn bootay de(r) ....
I should like a small packet of	**Je voudrais un petit paquet de ....** Zhe(r) voodray uh(n) pe(r)tee packay de(r) ....
Have you a larger one?	**En avez-vous de plus grand?** Ah(n) avay-voo de(r) plew grah(n)?
This is too large.	**C'est trop grand.** Say troh grah(n).

VOCABULARY

bag	**le sac**	le(r) sac
battery	**la pile**	la peel
corkscrew	**le tire-bouchon**	le(r) teer-booshoh(n)
cup	**la tasse**	la tass
detergent	**la lessive**	la lesseev
dishcloth	**le torchon**	le(r) torshoh(n)
disinfectant	**le désinfectant**	le(r) dayza(n)fectah(n)

fork	**la fourchette**	la foorshett
frying-pan	**la poêle**	la pwal
insect-repellant	**l'insecticide**	la(n)sectisseed
knife	**le couteau**	le(r) cootoh
matches	**les allumettes**	lez allewmett
needle	**l'aiguille**	laygwee
pan-scrubber (wire)	**l'éponge métallique**	laypoh(n)zh mettalleek
paraffin	**le pétrole**	le(r) paytrohl
plate	**l'assiette**	lassyett
peg	**la cheville**	la she(r)vee
saucepan	**la casserole**	la cassrol
saucer	**la soucoupe**	la soocoop
scissors	**les ciseaux**	lay seezoh
soap	**le savon**	le(r) savoh(n)
soap-powder	**le savon en poudre**	le(r) savoh(n) ah(n) poodr
spoon	**la cuiller**	la cweeyay
string	**la ficelle, la corde**	la feessell, la cord
tin	**la boîte**	la bwat
tin-opener	**l'ouvre-boîte**	loovr-bwaht
torch	**la lampe électrique**	la lah(n)p aylectreek
umbrella	**le parapluie**	le(r) paraplwee
wallet	**le portefeuille**	le(r) port-fe(r)y

4 Medicines and cosmetics

I want something for ...	**Je voudrais quelque chose pour ...** Zhe(r) voodray kelke(r) shohz poor ...
– constipation.	**– la constipation.** – la co(n)steepassyoh(n).
– diarrhoea.	**– la diarrhée.** – la deearray.
– a headache.	**– le mal de tête.** – le(r) mal de(r) tet.
– indigestion.	**– l'indigestion.** – la(n)deezhestyoh(n).

– stomach-ache.   **– le mal d'estomac.**
    – le(r) mal daystomah.

– a cold/cough.   **– le rhume/la toux.**
    – le(r) rewm/la too.

– a hangover.   **– la gueule de bois.**
    – la gerl de(r) bwa.

– car-sickness.   **– le mal de voiture.**
    – le(r) mal de(r) vwahtewr.

– sun-stroke.   **– l'insolation.**
    – la(n)solassyoh(n).

Have you anything for ...   **Avez-vous quelque chose pour ...**
    Avay-voo kelke(r) shohz poor ...

– insect-bites?   **– les piqûres d'insectes?**
    – lay peekewr da(n)sect?

– ant-bites?   **– les piqûres de fourmis?**
    – lay peekewr de(r) foormee?

– mosquito-bites?   **– les piqûres de moustiques?**
    – lay peekewr de(r) moosteek?

Can you please make up this prescription?   **Pouvez-vous faire cette ordonnance, s'il vous plaît?**
    Poovay-voo fair set ordonnah(n)ss, seelvooplay?

Do I need a prescription for this?   **Ai-je besoin d'une ordonnance pour acheter ceci?**
    Ayzh be(r)zwah(n) dewn ordonnah(n)ss poor ashtay se(r)ssee?

Shall I wait?   **J'attends?**
    Zhattah(n)?

When shall I come back?   **Quand est-ce que je dois rentrer?**
    Kah(n)t esske(r) zhe(r) dwah rah(n)tray?

*Come back in half an hour.   **Revenez dans une demi-heure.**
    Re(v)e(r)nay dah(n)z ewn de(r)mee-er.

*Come back at 3 o'clock.   **Revenez à trois heures.**
    Re(r)ve(r)nay a trwah zer.

How often should I take this?	**Combien de fois par jour dois-je prendre ceci?**
	Coh(n)byah(n) de(r) fwah par zhoor dwah-zh prah(n)dr se(r)ssee?
*Take . . .	**Prendre . . . .**
	Prah(n)dr . . .
– every three hours.	**– toutes les trois heures.**
	– toot lay trwaz er.
– four times a day.	**– quatre fois par jour.**
	– katr fwah par zhoor.
– after/before meals.	**– après/avant les repas.**
	– apray/avah(n) lay re(r)pah.
I am suffering from sunburn.	**J'ai attrapé un coup de soleil.**
	Zhay attrappay uh(n) coo de(r) solay.
I want cream, not oil.	**Je voudrais de la crême et non pas de l'huile.**
	Zhe voodray de(r) la crem, ay noh(n) pah de(r) lweel.
Do you sell contraceptives?	**Vendez-vous des contraceptifs?**
	Vah(n)day-voo day coh(n)trasepteef?
This lipstick is too dark/too pale.	**Ce rouge â lèvres est trop foncé/ trop pâle.**
	Se(r) roozh a levr ay troh foh(n)ssay/troh pahl.

GENERAL NOTICES

Mode d'emploi	Directions for use
L'usage externe	For external use only

VOCABULARY

after-shave lotion	**la lotion après-rasage** la lohssyoh(n) apray-razahzh
antiseptic cream	**la crème antiseptique** la crem ah(n)teesepteek
aspirin	**l'aspirine** laspireen
bandage	**la bande** la bah(n)d
(crepe)	**la bande Velpeau** la bah(n)d Velpoh
bathsalts	**les sels de bain** lay sel de(r) ba(n)
cleansing cream	**la lotion démaquillante** la lohssyoh(n) daymackeeyah(n)t
comb	**le peigne** le(r) paynj
cotton-wool	**l'ouate** lwaht
cough lozenges	**les pastilles contre la toux** lay pastee coh(n)tr la too
cosmetics	**les cosmetiques** lay cosmayteek
deodorant	**le déodorant** le(r) dayohdorah(n)
hair-brush	**la brosse à cheveux** la bross a she(r)ve(r)
hair-curler	**le bigoudi** le(r) beegoodee
laxative	**le laxatif** le(r) laxateef
lipstick	**le rouge à lèvres** le(r) roozh a levr
lotion	**la lotion** la lohssyoh(n)
medicine	**le médicament** le(r) maydeekamah(n)
nail-file	**la lime à ongles** la leem a oh(n)gl
nail-varnish	**le vernis à ongles** le(r) vairnee a oh(n)gl
nail-varnish remover	**le dissolvant** le(r) deesolvah(n)
perfume, bottle of	**le flacon de parfum** le(r) flacoh(n) de(r) parfuh(n)
powder	**la poudre** la poodr
powder-compact	**le poudrier** le(r) poodryay
prescription	**l'ordonnance** lordonnah(n)ss
razor	**le rasoir** le(r) razwahr
razor-blades	**les lames de rasoir** lay lahm de(r) razwahr
sanitary towels	**les serviettes hygièniques** lay sairvyetts eezhyeneek
shampoo	**le shampooing** le(r) shah(n)pwa(n)
shaving-brush	**le blaireau** le(r) blairoh

shaving-cream	**la crème à raser** la crem a razay
shaving-soap	**le savon à barbe** le(r) savoh(n) a barb
soap	**le savon** le(r) savoh(n)
sticking-plaster	**le sparadrap** le(r) sparadrah
sun glasses	**les lunettes de soleil** lay lewnett de(r) solay
suntan cream	**la crème solaire** la crem solair
talcum-powder	**le talc** le(r) talc
toilet paper	**le papier hygiènique** le(r) pappyay eezhyeneek
toothpaste	**le dentifrice** le(r) dah(n)teefreess
tooth-brush	**la brosse à dents** la bross a dah(n)

5 Photographic materials

I want a film of colour slides/of colour prints.	**Je voudrais une pellicule de diapositives en couleurs/ d'épreuves en couleurs.** Zhe(r) voodray ewn pellikewl de(r) deeapositeev ah(n) coole(r)/daypre(r)v ah(n) coole(r).
A 16/35 millimetre film.	**Seize/trente-cinq millimètres.** Sayz/trah(n)t-sank millimetr.
Twenty/thirty-six exposures.	**Vingt/trente-six poses.** Va(n)/trah(n)t-seess pohz.
I want a . . . film.	**Je voudrais une pellicule . . .** Zhe(r) voodray ewn pellikewl . . .
– black-and-white	**– en noir et blanc.** – ah(n) nwahr ay blah(n).
– fast	**– pour grande vitesse.** – poor grah(n)d veetess.
– slow	**– pour faible vitesse.** – poor faybl veetess.

Would you develop this film, please?	**Voulez-vous développer cette pellicule, s'il vous plait?**
	Voolay-voo dayvloppay set pellikewl, seelvooplay?
How much does it cost to develop?	**C'est combien pour le développement?**
	Say coh(n)byah(n) poor le(r) dayvlopmah(n)?
I want one print of each negative.	**Je voudrais une épreuve de chaque (cliché).**
	Zhe(r) voodray ewn aypre(r)v de(r) shack (clishay).
The film is stuck.	**La pellicule s'est coincée.**
	La pellikewl say cwa(n)say.
My camera doesn't work.	**Mon appareil ne marche pas.**
	Moh(n)n apparay ne(r) marsh pah.
When shall I come back?	**Quand est-ce que je dois revenir?**
	Kah(n)t-esske(r) zhe(r) dwah re(r)ve(r)neer?
*Come back tomorrow, please.	**Revenez demain, s'il vous plaît.**
	Re(r)ve(r)nay de(r)ma(n), seelvooplay.

6 Books and stationery

A bookshop is a **Librairie** and a stationer's a **Papeterie**. Most bookshops sell road maps and town plans. If you want an English magazine or newspaper, ask at a bookshop or news-stand **(kiosque).**

Have you any English newspapers?	**Avez-vous des journaux anglais?**
	Avay-voo day zhoornohz ah(n)glay?

*They will arrive this afternoon. **Ils arriveront cet après-midi.**
Eel zarreevroh(n) set
apray-meedee.

Do you have English books? **Avez-vous des livres anglais?**
Avay-voo day leevr zah(n)glay?

I want a blue biro. **Je voudrais un stylo à bille.**
Zhe(r) voodray uh(n) steelo a
beel.

A pad of writing-paper, please. **Un bloc de papier à écrire, s'il
vous plaît.**
Uh(n) bloc de(r) pappyay a
aycreer, seelvooplay.

Do you have a map of the town? **Avez-vous un plan de la ville?**
Avay-vooz uh(n) plah(n) de(r) la
veel?

Do you sell road maps? **Vendez-vous des cartes routières?**
Vah(n)day-voo day cart rootyair?

VOCABULARY

guidebook	**le guide**	le(r) geed
envelope	**l'enveloppe**	lahnvlop
ink	**l'encre**	lah(n)cr
magazine	**le magazine**	le(r) magazeen
novel	**le roman**	le(r) romah(n)
paperback	**le livre de poche**	le(r) leevr de(r) posh
pencil	**le crayon**	le(r) crayoh(n)
pen	**le stylo**	le(r) steelo
postcard	**la carte-postale**	la cart-postahl
rubber	**la gomme**	la gom

7 Cigarettes, tobacco and stamps

The main thing to remember is that you can buy stamps at a shop called a **café-tabac**, which looks just like an ordinary tobacconist.

A packet of . . ., please.	**Un paquet de . . ., s'il vous plaît.**
	Uh(n) packay de(r) . . ., seelvooplay.
Do you have any English cigarettes?	**Avez-vous des cigarettes anglaises?**
	Avay-voo day seegarett zah(n)glayz?
Filter tip/with no filter.	**A bout filtre/sans filtre.**
	A boo feeltr/sah(n)feeltr.
I want to buy a lighter.	**Je voudrais un briquet.**
	Zhe(r) voodray uh(n) breekay.
Do you sell lighter fuel?	**Vendez-vous de l'essence pour briquets?**
	Vah(n)day-voo de(r) lessah(n)ss poor breekay?
A box of matches, please.	**Une boîte d'allumettes, s'il vous plaît.**
	Ewn bwaht dallewmett, seelvooplay.
I want some stamps for a post-card to England.	**Je voudrais des timbres pour une carte-postale pour Angleterre.**
	Zhe(r) voodray day ta(n)br poor ewn cart-postahl poor Ah(n)gltair.
Two 30 centimes stamps, please.	**Deux timbres à trente centimes, s'il vous plaît.**
	De(r) ta(n)br a trah(n)t sah(n)teem, seelvooplay.

VOCABULARY

cigar	**le cigare** le(r) seegar
flint	**la pierre à briquet** la pyair a breekay
pipe	**la pipe** la peep
pipe-cleaner	**le cure-pipe** le(r) cure-peep
tobacco	**le tabac** le(r) tabah

General notices

Soldes	Sale
Vente de soldes	Clearance sale
Prix de soldes	Bargain prices
Entrée libre	No obligation to buy
Caisse	Cash-desk
Libre-service	Self-service
Ici on parle anglais	English spoken
Ascenseur	Lift
Sortie	Way out
Ouverte de . . . à . . . h	Open from . . . to . . . o'clock

At the Hairdresser

Women A shampoo and set is **un shampooing et une mise en plis.**

Men An ordinary trim is **une coupe ordinaire.** If you want a razor-cut (**une coupe de rasoir**) you will have to have either a shampoo first or else hair-paraffin treatment (**pétrole**) in order to wet the hair.

I should like to make an appointment for three o'clock.	**Je voudrais prendre un rendez-vous pour trois heures.** Zhe(r) voodray prah(n)dr uh(n) rah(n)day-voo poor trwahz er.
I should like a shampoo and set.	**Je voudrais un shampooing et une mise en plis.** Zhe(r) voodray uh(n) shah(n)pwa(n) ay ewn meez ah(n) plee.
I want my hair . . .	**Voulez-vous me . . . les cheveux, s'il vous plaît?** Voolay-voo me(r) . . . lay she(r)ve(r), seelvooplay?
– cut.	**– couper** – coopay
– trimmed.	**– rafraichir** – rafraysheer
– tinted.	**– colorer** – coloray
– washed.	**– laver** – lavay
Please don't cut it too short.	**Ne les coupez pas trop courts.** Ne(r) lay coopay pah troh coor.

Can you take a bit more off?	**Pouvez-vous couper encore un peu, s'il vous plaît?**
	Poovay-voo coopay ah(n)cor uh(n) pe(r), seelvooplay?
I should like some setting-lotion/ some conditioner.	**Je voudrais un fixateur pour mise en plis/un baume embellisseur.**
	Zhe(r) voodray uh(n) feexater poor meez ah(n) plee/ewn bohm ah(n)belleesser.
I want a shave.	**Je voudrais qu'on me rase.**
	Zhe(r) voodray koh(n) me(r) raz.
I should like a manicure.	**Je voudrais qu'on me fasse les ongles.**
	Zhe(r) voodray koh(n) me(r) fass lez oh(n)gl.
Thank you. I like it.	**Merci. C'est très bien.**
	Mairssee. Say tray byah(n).

At the Bank

Once in France you can change your currency or traveller's cheques into francs at customs exchange offices, recognised banks or officially authorised hotels.

To change traveller's cheques you need to produce your passport. The rate of exchange varies, but it is normally displayed prominently inside the bank or **bureau de change**. A small commission is charged, so you never get quite as much as the rate advertised.

Hours You will find that in most large towns the banking hours are Monday to Friday from 9.00 a.m. to 12.00 a.m. and from 2.00 p.m. to 4.00 p.m., but closed on Saturdays and Sundays. However, in the provinces they are generally open from Tuesdays to Saturdays from 9.00 a.m. to 12.00 a.m. and from 2.00 p.m. to 4.00 p.m., but closed on Sundays and Mondays. Banks are closed on national holidays, a list of which is given on p. 137.

Where is the nearest bank?
(*See* 'Directions' (p. 17) *for possible answers.*)

Où se trouve la banque la plus proche?
Oo se(r) troov la bah(n)k la plew prosh?

Where is the nearest currency exchange?

Où se trouve le bureau de change le plus proche?
Oo se(r) troov le(r) buro de(r) shah(n)zh le(r) plew prosh?

Can I cash a traveller's cheque here?

Puis-je encaisser un chèque de voyage ici?
Pwee-zh ah(n)caissay uh(n) shek de(r) vwa-yahzh eessee?

Do you accept traveller's cheques? **Acceptez-vous les chèques de voyage?**
Acceptay-voo lay shek de(r) vwa-yahzh?

How much do I get for the pound/dollar? **Combien vaut la livre/le dollar?**
Coh(n)byah(n) voh la leevr/le(r) dolar?

How much commission do you charge? **Combien prenez-vous pour votre commission?**
Coh(n)bya(n) pre(r)nay-voo poor votr commeessyoh(n)?

Can you give me some small change? **Pourriez-vous me donner de la monnaie?**
Poorryay-voo me(r) donnay de(r) la monnay?

I have a letter of credit. **J'ai une lettre de crédit.**
Zhay ewn letr de(r) craydee.

At the Post Office

The French Post Office – the PTT (**Postes, Télégraphes, Téléphones**) – is generally open from 8.00 a.m. to 7.00 p.m. on Mondays to Fridays, and from 8.00 a.m. to 12.00 a.m. on Saturdays.

Post boxes, which are usually yellow, can be found outside post offices and in the street, often near a café. Collection times are displayed, and it is worth looking at these, as some boxes are only cleared once a week. There are sometimes separate boxes for letters (**lettres**) and printed matter (**imprimés**), and main post offices may have a box marked '**avion**' (air mail).

The various counters, or **guichets**, at a post office are for money orders (**mandats**), telegrams (**télégrammes**), savings bank (**caisse d'épargne**), stamps (**timbres-poste**), parcels (**paquets**), telephone discs (**jetons**), personal mail (**poste restante**). Stamps can also be purchased from the stamp-machines outside, and from cafés. In order to cash a money order or collect your poste restante, you will need to show your passport or identity card. You will probably be charged a few centimes for this service.

Where is the main post office, please?	**Où est le bureau principal des PTT, s'il vous plaît?** Oo ay le(r) buro prah(n)seepal day pay-tay-tay, seelvooplay?
What time does it open?	**A quelle heure ouvre-t-il?** A kel er oovr-teel?
Where is the nearest post office?	**Où est le bureau de poste le plus proche?** Oo ay le(r) buro de(r) post le(r) plew prosh?

Where can I find a post box?	**Où puis-je trouver une boîte aux lettres?**
	Oo pweezh troovay ewn bwat oh lettr?
How much is a stamp for England?	**Quel est le prix d'un timbre pour l'Angleterre?**
	Kel ay le(r) pree duh(n) ta(n)br poor lAh(n)gltair?
It's for a letter/postcard.	**C'est pour une lettre/carte postale.**
	Say poor ewn lettr/cart postahl.
I would like three stamps for letters/postcards to England.	**Je voudrais trois timbres pour des lettres/cartes postales pour l'Angleterre.**
	Zhe(r) voodray trwa ta(n)br poor day lettr/cart postahl poor lAh(n)gltair.
Give me five . . . centimes stamps.	**Donnez-moi cinq timbres à . . . centimes.**
	Donnay-mwa sank tah(n)br a . . . sah(n)teem.
A book of stamps, please.	**Un carnet de timbres, s'il vous plaît.**
	Uh(n) carnay de(r) tah(n)br, seelvooplay.
I want to send an express letter to London.	**Je veux envoyer une lettre express à Londres.**
	Zhe(r) ve(r) ah(n)vwayay ewn lettr express a Loh(n)dr.
I want to send this to Edinburgh by recorded delivery.	**Je veux envoyer ceci à Edimbourg avec accusé de réception.**
	Zhe(r) ve(r) ah(n)vwayay se(r)see a Ayda(n)boor avec accewzay de(r) raysepssyoh(n).
Can I register this package, please?	**Puis-je faire recommander ce paquet, s'il vous plaît?**
	Pweezh fair recommah(n)day se(r) packay, seelvooplay?

How much will it cost to send this parcel to Brighton?

Quel est l'affranchissage de ce colis pour Brighton?

Kel ay laffrah(n)sheessahzh de(r) se(r) collee poor Breetoh(n)?

I want to send a telegram to Birmingham in England.

Je voudrais envoyer un télégramme à Birmingham en Angleterre.

Zhe(r) voodray ah(n)vwayay uh(n) taylaygram a Beermeengham ahnAh(n)gltair.

*Please fill in this form.

Remplissez cette formule, s'il vous plaît.

Rah(n)pleessay set formewl, seelvooplay.

How much is it per word?

Quel est le prix par mot?

Kel ay le(r) pree par moh?

Reply paid, please.

Réponse payée, s'il vous plaît.

Raypoh(n)ss payay, seelvooplay.

Where is the poste restante counter?

Où se trouve le guichet de poste restante?

Oo se(r) troov le(r) geeshay de(r) post restahnt?

Is there any post for me?

Y a-t-il du courrier pour moi?

Yateel dew coorryay poor mwa?

I am expecting a money order. Where should I go?

J'attends un mandat. Où faut-il aller?

Zhattah(n)zuh(n) mah(n)dah. Oo foh-teel allay?

I want to cash a money order.

Je veux encaisser un mandat.

Zhe(r) ve(r) ah(n)kaissay uh(n) mah(n)dah.

I want to send some money to . . . .

Je voudrais envoyer de l'argent en . . . .

Zhe(r) voodray ah(n)vwayay de(r) larzhah(n) ah(n) . . . .

What time does the next/last post leave?	**A quelle heure a lieu la prochaine/ dernière levée de courrier?**
	A kel er a lye(r) la proshen/ dairnyay levay de(r) coorryay?
When is the next delivery?	**A quelle heure est la prochaine distribution?**
	A kel er ay la proshen deestreebyoussyoh(n)?
Can you forward my mail?	**Pourriez-vous faire suivre mon courrier?**
	Poorryay-voo fair sweevr moh(n) coorryay?

The Telephone

Public call boxes are few and far between in France, and most 'phone calls are made either from a post office or from a café. Post offices have blue, yellow and black telephones. The blue ones are for local calls and operate either by coins or by special telephone discs, called **jetons**, which can be bought at the telephone counter of the post office or in a cafe. Yellow 'phones are for local or long-distance calls and take coins only. Black phones are for long-distance and international calls. You have to give the number you want to the operator, who will make the connection and tell you which booth to go to.

The numbers shown on the dial of automatic telephones are:

renseignements	enquiries
réclamations	'phone out of order
télégraphe	telegrams
police-secours	police
pompiers	fire brigade

Is there a 'phone in this café?	**Y a-t-il un téléphone dans ce café?** Yateel uh(n) taylayphon dah(n) se(r) caffay?
May I use the 'phone?	**Puis-je me servir du téléphone?** Pweezh me(r) sairveer dew taylayphon?
Where can I find a 'phone box?	**Où puis-je trouver une cabine téléphonique?** Oo pweezh troovay ewn cabeen taylayphoneek?
Please give me two tokens for the 'phone.	**Donnez-moi deux jetons de téléphone, s'il vous plaît.** Donnay-mwa de(r) zhetoh(n) de(r) taylayphon, seelvooplay.

I want to make a person-to-person call to	**Je veux appeler avec préavis à ....**
	Zhe(r) ve(r) appellay avec prayavee a ....
I want to make a reverse charge call to	**Je veux téléphoner en p.c.v. à ....**
	Zhe(r) ve(r) taylayphonay ah(n) pay-say-vay a ....
*What's your number?	**Quel est votre numéro?**
	Kel ay votr newmairoh?
How much does it cost to 'phone to ...?	**Quel est le prix d'une communication téléphonique pour ...?**
	Kel ay le(r) pree dewn commewneekassyoh(n) taylayphoneek poor ...?
Get me ..., please.	**Donnez-moi ..., s'il vous plaît.**
	Donnay-mwa ..., seelvooplay.
*You can dial direct to Bordeaux.	**Vous pouvez appeler Bordeaux en automatique.**
	Voo poovay appellay Bordoh ahnohtohmateek.
I want to make a 'phone call to England. The number is Bristol 25608.	**Je veux téléphoner en Angleterre. Le numéro est Bristol vingt-cinq mille six cent huit.**
	Zhe(r) ve(r) taylayphonay ahnAh(n)gltair. Le(r) newmairoh ay Breestol va(n)-sank meel see sah(n) weet.
*Don't put the receiver down.	**Ne raccrochez pas**
	Ne(r) raccroshay pah.
How much will it cost for three minutes?	**Combien coûteront trois minutes?**
	Combya(n) cooteroh(n) trwa meenewt?
*Hold the line.	**Ne quittez pas.**
	Ne(r) keetay pah.
*The line is engaged.	**La ligne est occupée.**
	La leenj aytoccewpay.

*There's no reply.
Il n'y a pas de réponse.
Eelnya pah de(r) raypoh(n)ss.

I'll try again later.
Je rappellerai plus tard.
Zhe(r) rappelleray plew tar.

*Who's speaking?
Qui est à l'appareil?
Kee ayta lapparay?

Extension 400, please.
Poste quatre cent, s'il vous plaît.
Post katr sah(n), seelvooplay.

I want to speak to Mr Watson.
**Je voudrais parler à Monsieur
     Watson.**
Zhe(r) voodray parlay a
     Me(r)syer Watson.

*He isn't in at present.
Il n'est pas là pour le moment.
Eel nay pah la poor le(r)
     momah(n).

*You've got the wrong number.
Vous vous êtes trompé de numéro.
Voo voozet troh(n)pay de(r)
     newmairoh.

Tell him/her that . . . 'phoned.
Dites-lui que . . . a téléphoné.
Deet-lwee ke(r) . . . a taylayphonay.

Ask him/her to ring me at . . . ,
     please.
**Demandez-lui de me rappeler à . . . ,
     s'il vous plaît.**
Demah(n)day-lwee de(r) me(r)
     rappellay a . . . , seelvooplay.

Do you speak English?
Parlez-vous anglais?
Parlay-voo ah(n)glay?

*You are wanted on the 'phone.
On vous demande au téléphone.
Oh(n) voo demah(n)d oh
     taylayphon.

I have been cut off.
La communication a été coupée.
La commewneekassyoh(n) a
     aytay coopay.

Please reconnect me.
Veuillez la rétablir.
Ve(r)yay la raytableer.

This 'phone is not working.
Cet appareil ne fonctionne pas.
Set apparay ne(r) fonkssyon
     pah.

Useful information and addresses

To make the most of your stay in Paris, you should pay a visit to the Office de Tourisme de Paris (the Paris Tourist Office), 127 avenue des Champs-Élysées, Paris 8e. Here you will be able to change your money and traveller's cheques, reserve hotel rooms in Paris and elsewhere in France, and obtain completely up-to-date information about where to go and what to see – and there is always someone there who speaks English.

The Tourist Office will be able to give you a complete list of the many theatres, exhibitions, concerts, museums, art galleries and places of interest. You are also advised to check with them on opening and closing hours, admission prices and so on, as these tend to vary. You should bear in mind that a number of museums and monuments are closed on Tuesdays.

The Office de Tourisme de Paris is open daily from 9.00 a.m. to midnight.

Young people and students looking for accommodation should contact:

> Centre de Documentation et d'Information pour la Jeunesse
> 101 quai Banly
> Paris 75015

or

> Service Parisien d'Accueil aux Étudiants Étrangers
> 6 rue Jean-Calvin
> Paris 75005

It is sometimes possible for students to find accommodation at the Cité Universitaire, and information is obtainable from:

Service Administratif de la Cité Internationale de l'Université
de Paris
19 boulevard Jourdan
Paris 75014

For information on youth hostels, please see the relevant
section (p. 50).

Travel

The easiest and most convenient method of transport for
foreigners in Paris is the metro. Unlike the Underground in
London, there is a flat-rate fare, and a small saving is made if a
carnet of ten tickets is bought. The metro runs from 5.30 a.m. to
1.15 a.m.

There are two new 'express' lines from Auber to Saint-
Germain-en-Laye and from Nation to Boissy-Saint-Léger. Each
journey takes fifteen minutes.

Buses run from 6.30 a.m. to 8.30 and 9.30 p.m. (and in some
cases until 12.30 a.m.). Details of days and times are displayed
on bus stops. Bus and metro tickets are interchangeable and the
price of your bus ride depends on how many zones (or 'sections')
you cross. In Paris, this will be either one or two. You should
ring the bell when you want to get off the bus.

Tickets for foreign tourists

These 'go-as-you-please' tickets allow unlimited journeys to
foreigners during a given period, and can be bought at the Paris
Tourist Office and at a number of major metro stations.

Currency exchange

Banks in Paris are open from 9.00 a.m. to 4.30 p.m. Monday to Friday and are closed on public holidays, a list of which is to be found at the back of this book. They are also closed for half a day preceding a public holiday. Currency exchange offices are generally open on Saturday mornings, and you will find exchange offices open until late every day (including Sunday) at the Gare d'Austerlitz, Gare de l'Est, Gare de Lyon, Gare Saint-Lazare, Charles de Gaulle, Orly and Le Bourget airports, the Aérogare (airport terminal) des Invalides, and the Tourist Office in the Champs Élysées.

Post office services

Post offices are open daily from 8.00 a.m. to 7.00 p.m. and on Saturday mornings from 8.00 a.m. to 12.00 a.m. The main post office in Paris is at 52 rue du Louvre, Paris 75001. The following post offices are open twenty-four hours a day for telephone and telegraph services:

8 place de la Bourse, Paris 75002
103 rue du Louvre, Paris 75001

A special postal service in Paris is the pneumatic system. Letters posted in the pneumatic boxes in post offices arrive at their destinations in under three hours.

Shops

The large department stores in Paris are all within easy reach of one another, and are open from 9.30 a.m. to 6.30 p.m. Some of the most popular are:

Aux Grands Magasins du Louvre (Place du Palais Royal, Paris 75001)

> Au Printemps (69 boulevard Haussman, Paris 75009)
> Galeries Lafayette (40 boulevard Haussman, Paris 75009)
> Aux Trois Quartiers (17 boulevard de la Madeleine, Paris 75001)
> Au Bon Marché (22 rue de Sèvres, Paris 75007)

All the large stores have snack bars and cheap restaurants, usually with a set menu, where you can eat quite well. There is also tax-free shopping for foreigners, on production of your passport.

The French equivalent of Bond Street is the faubourg Saint-Honoré, the avenue Victor Hugo, the avenue Montaigne and the rue de Passy, where small modern shops sell luxury goods.

If you are interested in antiques, you should pay a visit to the Marché aux Puces (flea market) between the Porte de Saint-Ouen and Porte de Clignancourt, or to the faubourgs Saint-Honoré, Saint-Germain and Le Marais.

The open-air stamp market at the corner of avenue Gabriel and avenue Marigny is open on Saturdays, Sundays and Thursday afternoons.

Some of the many famous markets are the rue Mouffetard (food), rue de Buci and carreau de temple (second-hand goods). At Place Louis-Lépine there is a flower market, and on Sundays a bird market. The largest market in the world, Les Halles, has now moved to Rungis – information obtainable from the Syndicat d'Initiative des Halles de Rungis.

For children there are puppet shows in the Jardin des Champs Élysées (avenue Gabriel) and the Jardin de Luxembourg (boulevard Saint-Michel).

Among the many parks and gardens, some of the most famous are the Bois de Boulogne with its seven lakes, the Jardin de Luxembourg (metro: Gare de Lyon) and the Jardin des Plantes (metro: Austerlitz).

Sightseeing

The French equivalent to a tourist information office is the **Syndicat d'Initiative**, sometimes called an **Office de Tourisme**. They are usually very helpful and will supply you with lists of hotels and restaurants, timetables, town plans and details of local excursions, and will answer all your enquiries. Most towns have a **syndicat**, but they differ considerably in size and in the service they provide. Hours of opening vary, but you will generally find them open between 9.00 a.m. and 12.00 a.m. and between 2.00 p.m. and 6.00 p.m. In general, you should expect to have to pay an entrance fee to places of interest. If you go into a church or cathedral, remember to be decently dressed; this is less important than it used to be, but it is still the case that you may not be allowed in if your arms and legs are not suitably covered.

Where is the information office?
(*For possible answers, see pp. 17–18*)

Où se trouve le syndicat d'initiative?
Oo se(r) troov le(r) sa(n)deeca dinissyateev?

Where can I buy a map of the town?

Où puis-je acheter un plan de la ville?
Oo pweezh ashtay uh(n) plah(n) de(r) la veel?

*You must go to a bookshop.

Il faut aller à une librairie.
Eel foht allay a ewn leebrairi.

What is there of interest to see?

Qu'est-ce qu'il y a d'intéressant?
Kesskeelya da(n)tairessah(n)?

Where is the old part of the town?

Où se trouve le vieux quartier de la ville?
Oo se(r) troov le(r) vye(r) kartyay de(r) la veel?

Can you tell me the way to . . . ?	**Pouvez-vous m'indiquer le chemin pour . . . ?** Poovay-voo ma(n)deekay le(r) she(r)ma(n) poor . . . ?
(For possible answers, see pp. 17-18) How much is the admission charge ?	**Quel est le tarif d'entrée ?** Kel ay le(r) tareef dah(n)tray ?
Is there a reduction for students ?	**Y a-t-il un tarif réduit pour étudiants ?** Yateel uh(n) tareef raydwee poor aytewdyah(n) ?
Can we go round it ?	**Peut-on faire la visite ?** Pertoh(n) fair la viseet ?
*The next tour is at two o'clock.	**La prochaine visite est à deux heures.** La proshayn viseet ayt a de(r)z er.
Is there an English-speaking guide ?	**Y a-t-il un guide qui parle anglais ?** Yateel uh(n) geed kee parl ah(n)glay ?
*Please follow the guide.	**Suivez le guide, s'il vous plaît.** Sweevay le(r) geed, seelvooplay.
How much is the guidebook/ postcard ?	**Quel est le prix du guide/de la carte postale ?** Kel ay le(r) pree dew geed/de(r) la cart postahl ?
May I take photographs ?	**Est-ce que c'est permis de prendre des photos ?** Esske(r) say pairmee de(r) prah(n)dr day fohtoh ?
*Cameras are prohibited.	**Les appareils photographiques sont interdits.** Lez aparay fohtohgrafeek soh(n)t a(n)tairdee.

I should like to go on a tour (of the region).

Je voudrais faire un voyage organisé (dans la région).
Zhe(r) voodray fair uh(n) vwa-yahzh organeezay (dah(n) la rayzhyoh(n)).

Can I book it here?

Peut-on réserver la place ici?
Pertoh(n) raysairvay la plass eessee?

How much does the tour cost?

Quel est le prix du voyage?
Kel ay le(r) pree dew va-yahzh?

When does the coach leave?

A quelle heure part l'autocar?
A kel er par lohtohcar?

Where does the coach leave from?

D'où part l'autocar?
Doo par lohtohcar?

How long does it take?

Le voyage prend combien de temps?
Le(r) vwa-yahzh prah(n) combyah(n) de(r) te(n)?

Ententainments

Performances at cinemas, theatres, concerts, etc. often begin rather late in France.

Cinemas usually open from 9.00 to 11.00 p.m. on weekdays, and at approximately 2.30, 5.30 and 9.30 p.m. at weekends. There is generally only one main film, and larger cinemas have continuous performances.

In cinemas and theatres, smoking is forbidden, and one is expected to tip the usherette. Programmes are on sale before the performance begins, and during the interval.

Some of the following phrases can, of course, be used on visits to football matches and other spectator sports.

What's on at the cinema/theatre/ opera?

Qu'est-ce qu'on joue/au cinéma/ au théâtre/à l'opéra?
Kesskoh(n) zhoo oh seenaymah/ oh tayatr/a lopayrah?

Is there a ballet/concert on tonight?

Est-ce qu'il y a un ballet/concert ce soir?
Esskeelya uh(n) ballay/coh(n)sair se(r) swahr?

What's the programme?

Qu'y a-t-il au programme?
Kyateel oh program?

Who is playing . . . ?

Qui joue le rôle de . . . ?
Kee zhoo le(r) rol de(r) . . . ?

Who is the director?

Qui est le metteur en scène?
Kee ay le(r) metter ah(n)sen?

Who are the singers?

Quels sont les chanteurs?
Kel soh(n) lay shah(n)ter?

Who are the dancers?

Quels sont les danseurs?
Kel soh(n) lay dah(n)ser?

Which orchestra is it?	**Quel est l'orchestre?**
	Kel ay lorkestr?
Who is the conductor?	**Qui est le chef d'orchestre?**
	Kee ay le(r) shef dorkestr?
What sort of film/play is it?	**C'est quel genre de film/pièce?**
	Say kel zhah(n)r de(r) feelm/ pyess?
*It's a thriller/comedy/tragedy/ musical/review.	**C'est un policier/une comédie/ une tragédie/une comédie musicale/une revue.**
	Sayt uh(n) poleessyer/ewn comaydee/ewn trazhaydee/ ewn comaydee mewzeekal/ ewn revew.
What time does the programme begin/end?	**A quelle heure commence/se termine le spectacle?**
	A kel er commah(n)ss/se(r) tairmeen le(r) spektahkl?
Is there a matinee?	**Y a-t-il une matinée?**
	Yateel ewn mateenay?
Is there a performance today/on Sunday?	**Est-ce qu'il y a une présentation aujourd'hui/dimanche?**
	Esskeelya ewn praysah(n)tassyoh(n) ohzhoordwee/deemah(n)sh?
Is the film dubbed, or are there sub-titles?	**Est-ce que le film est doublé, ou y a-t-il des sous-titres?**
	Esske(r) le(r) feelm ay dooblay, oo yateel day soo-teetr?
How much are the tickets?	**A combien sont les tickets?**
	A combya(n) soh(n) lay teekay?
Can one book seats?	**Peut-on louer des places?**
	Pe(r)toh(n) looay day plass?

Have you anything cheaper?

Avez-vous quelque chose de moins cher?

Avay-voo kelke(r)shoze de(r) mwa(n) shair?

Do you have reductions for students/children/groups?

Avez-vous des réductions pour étudiants/enfants/groupes?

Avay-voo day raydewkssyoh(n) poor aytewdyah(n)/ ah(n)fah(n)/groop?

*Children are not admitted.

Les enfants ne sont pas admis.

Laze ah(n)fah(n) ne(r) soh(n) pahzadmee.

Four tickets in the stalls for tomorrow, please.

Donnez-moi quatre places d'orchestre pour demain, s'il vous plaît.

Donnay-mwa katr plass dorkestr poor dema(n), seelvooplay.

*I am afraid all the tickets are sold.

Je regrette toutes les places sont vendues.

Zhe(r) regret toot lay plass soh(n) vah(n)dew.

Two in the circle, please.

Deux balcons, s'il vous plaît.

De(r) balkoh(n), seelvooplay.

A programme, please.

Un programme, s'il vous plaît.

Uh(n) program, seelvooplay.

Is there . . . in this town?

Y a-t-il . . . dans cette ville?

Yateel . . . dah(n) set veel?

– a dance-hall

– un dancing

– uh(n) dah(n)seeng

– a jazz club

– un club de jazz

– uh(n) klyoub de(r) zhazz

– a circus

– un cirque

– uh(n) seerk

– a zoo

– un zoo

– uh(n) zoo

– a night club

– une boîte de nuit

– ewn bwat de(r) nwee

– a casino

– un casino
– uh(n) casino

Where is it ?

Où se trouve-t-il?
Oo se(r) troov-teel ?

NOTICE

Interdit au moins de 18 ans

No children under 18 admitted

On the beach

France is, of course, famous for her beaches, not only on the fashionable Riviera but also on her Atlantic coastline; some of her finest beaches, especially for families, are to be found in Normandy and Brittany. In some parts, particularly along the crowded Mediterranean coast, a small charge is made for admission onto the beaches. In most resorts there are 'beach clubs' which organise supervised activities and games for children, and sometimes for their parents as well.

Where is the nearest beach?	**Où est la plage la plus proche?**
	Oo ay la plahzh la plew prosh?
Is it sand or shingle?	**Est-ce de sable ou de galets?**
	Ess de(r) sahbl oo de(r) galay?
Is there another beach?	**Est-ce qu'il y a une autre plage?**
	Esskeelya ewn ohtr plahzh?
Is it safe for swimming?	**Est-ce que la baignade est sans danger?**
	Esske(r) la baynjahd ay sah(n) dah(n)zhay?
Is it safe for children to swim?	**Est-ce que les enfants peuvent se baigner en sécurité?**
	Esske(r) laze ah(n)fah(n) pe(r)v se(r) baynjay ah(n) saycewreetay?
Can one go water-skiing/surfing here?	**Peut-on faire du ski nautique/surfing ici?**
	Pe(r)-toh(n) fair dew skee nohteek/sewrfeeng eessee?
I would like to hire ...	**Je voudrais louer ...**
	Zhe(r) voodray looay ...

– a cabin.	– **une cabine.**
	– ewn cabeen.
– a deck chair.	– **une chaise longue.**
	– ewn shayz loh(n)g.
– a sunshade.	– **un parasol.**
	– uh(n) parasol.
– a surf board.	– **une planche de surfing.**
	– ewn plah(n)sh de(r) sewrfeeng.
– some water-skis.	– **des skis nautiques.**
	– day skee nohteek.

NOTICES

Défense de se baigner No bathing
Plage privée Private beach

NB It is not safe to bathe when there is a red flag flying.

Fishing

Fishing is an extremely popular sport in France. Normandy and Brittany, the mountains in the centre of the country, the Alps and the Pyrenees are all good trout-fishing areas. Pike is found in abundance in the slower-moving rivers, and salmon in the rivers of Brittany, the Loire and the fast-moving streams of the Basque country.

Rivers, waterways and lakes are divided into those of first and second category (trout and coarse fishing respectively) and also into those which are State owned and those which are privately owned. There are fewer strictly private rivers in France than in Britain, but it is advisable to join a local angling club in order to find out about the places to fish and the different baits and flies.

For river and lake fishing the law requires you to be a paid-up member of an anglers' association (**une association de pêche et de pisciculture**) recognised by the regional **Prefêt**. Membership cards are issued by anglers' associations and by fishing-tackle shops. A list of addresses in France of the Associations is available from the French Government Tourist Office in London.

For sea fishing from the shore no permit is required for a hand-held rod or line, but when fishing from a boat you will have to obtain a navigation permit (**rôle de plaisance** or **carte de circulation**) from the local marine authority. More information about the rules for sea fishing and underwater fishing is available from the **Administrateurs Chefs des Quartiers d'Inscription Maritime**.

Is one allowed to fish here?	**Est-il permis de pêcher ici?**
	Ayt-eel pairmee de(r) peshay eessee?
Must one have a permit?	**Faut-il avoir un permis?**
	Foht-eel avwahr uh(n) pairmee?
Where can I get a permit?	**Où peut-on obtenir un permis?**
	Oo pert-oh(n) obte(r)neer uh(n) pairmee?
What is the maximum catch allowable?	**Quelle est la prise maximum permise?**
	Kel ay la preez maxeemum pairmeez?
Do I have to pay dues?	**Faut-il payer des droits de pêche?**
	Foht-eel payay day drwah de(r) pesh?
Can you recommend a good place to fish?	**Pourriez-vous me recommender un bon endroit pour pêcher?**
	Pooryay-voo me(r) re(r)commah(n)day uh(n) boh(n) nah(n)drwah poor peshay?

I should like to hire a fishing boat/ fishing rod.	**Je voudrais louer un bateau de pêche/une canne à pêche.**
	Zhe(r) voodray looay uh(n) battoh de(r) pesh/ewn can a pesh.
Can one go deep-sea fishing?	**Peut-on aller pêcher en pleine mer?**
	Pert-oh(n) allay peshay ah(n) playn mair?
You have a good catch.	**Vous faites une bonne pêche.**
	Voo fet ewn bonn pesh.

Ski-ing and Climbing

Alpine sports, particularly skiing, have rapidly grown in popularity in France and many new ski resorts have been developed in the French Alps in recent years. Actual resorts differ considerably in sophistication, chic and expense, but nearly all have ski schools with English-speaking instructors, and ski equipment available for hire.

Where is the ski school?	**Où se trouve l'école de ski?**
	Oo se(r) troov laycoll de(r) skee?
I am a fairly experienced skier/ climber.	**Je suis un skieur/alpiniste assez experimenté.**
	Zhe(r) swee uh(n) skeeyer/ alpeeneest assay expereemah(n)tay.
Can one hire skis here?	**Peut-on louer des skis ici?**
	Pert-oh(n) looay day skeez eessee?
Where can I buy/hire skis and sticks?	**Où peut-on acheter/louer des skis et des batons de ski?**
	Oo pert-oh(n) ashtay/looay day skee ay day battoh(n) de(r) skee?

I want to hire ski-boots.

Je voudrais louer des bottes de ski.
Zhe(r) voodray looay day bott de(r) skee.

I should like a weekly/monthly abonnement.

Je voudrais un abonnement pour une semaine/pour un mois.
Zhe(r) voodray uh(n) abbonnmah(n) poor ewn se(r)mayn/poor uh(n) mwa.

Is there a guide here?

Y a-t-il un guide ici?
Yateel uh(n) geed eessee?

I am worried about my friend.

Je m'inquiète à cause de mon ami.
Zhe(r) ma(n)keeyet a cohz de(r) moh(n) nammee.

He has not returned.

Il n'est pas encore rentré.
Eel nay pahz ah(n)cor rah(n)tray.

He has broken a leg.

Il s'est cassé la jambe.
Eel say cassay la zhah(n)b.

He has fallen.

Il est tombé.
Eel ay toh(n)bay.

Other games and sports

Is there a swimming pool/tennis club near here?

Y a-t-il une piscine/un club de tennis près d'ici?
Yateel ewn peesseen/uh(n) club de(r) te(r)nees pray deesee?

Where is the nearest . . . ?

Où est le . . . le plus proche?
Oo ay le(r) . . . le(r) plew prosh?

*There isn't one here.

Il n'y en a pas ici.
Eel nyah(n) a pahz eessee.

*The nearest one is at . . . .

Le plus proche est à . . . .
Le(r) plew prosh ayt a . . . .

Is the pool heated?

L'eau est-elle chauffée?
Loh ayt-ell shohfay?

Is it an open-air pool?

La piscine est en plein air?
La peesseen ayt ah(n) playnair?

I should like to hire	**Je voudrais louer ....** Zhe(r) voodray looay ....
How much does it cost for the hour/the day/the week?	**Quel est le tarif pour une heure/ la journée/ la semaine?** Kel ay le(r) tareef poor ewn er/ la zhoornay/la se(r)mayn?
Do I have to join the club?	**Faut-il devenir membre?** Foht-eel de(r)ve(r)neer mah(n)br?
What time does it open/close?	**A quelle heure ouvre-t-il/ ferme-t-il?** A kel er oovr-teel/fairm-teel?
When is the next race meeting?	**Quelle est la date des prochaines courses?** Kel ay la dat day proshayn coorss?
Who is the favourite?	**Qui est le favori?** Kee ay le(r) favvoree?
Twenty francs each way on	**Vingt francs à gagner et à perdre sur ....** Va(n) frah(n) a ganjay ay a pairdr soor ....
Twenty francs to win on	**Vingt francs à gagner sur ....** Va(n) frah(n) a ganjay soor ....
I should like some lessons.	**Je voudrais prendre des leçons.** Zhe(r) voodray prah(n)dr day le(r)ssoh(n).
I am a beginner.	**Je suis débutant.** Zhe(r) swee daybewtah(n).

VOCABULARY

ball (tennis)	**la balle**	la bal
(football)	**le ballon**	le(r) balloh(n)
boat	**le bateau**	le(r) battoh
motor	**le canot-automobile**	le(r) cannoh-ohtohmobeel

sailing	**le bateau à voiles** le(r) battoh a vwahl
with outboard engine	**le hors-bord** le or-bor
club	**le club** le(r) club
game	**la partie** la partee
golf course	**le golf** le(r) golf
ice-rink	**la patinoire** la patteenwahr
ice-skates	**les patins** lay patta(n)
horse	**le cheval** le(r) she(r)vahl
match	**le match** le(r) match
racecourse	**le terrain de courses** le(r) terra(n) de(r) coorss
races	**les courses** lay coorss
riding school	**le manège** le(r) mannayzh
swimming costume	**le maillot de bain** le(r) mayoh de(r) ba(n)
swimming pool	**la piscine** la peesseen
tennis racket	**la raquette** la rackett

Health

In urgent cases and for hospital treatment, residents of all Common Market countries are entitled to the same medical privileges as nationals, when refunds of 70% to 80% are likely to be obtained. Ask your Department of Health and Social Security for leaflet SA28.

This agreement does not cover minor ailments, and if you think you may need to see a doctor or dentist while on holiday you are advised to take out medical insurance, as treatment must be paid for on the spot.

At the doctor's

I need to see a doctor.

Il me faut voir un médecin.
Eel me(r) foh vwahr uh(n) maidsa(n).

Is there a doctor here who speaks English?

Y a-t-il un médecin ici qui parle anglais?
Yateel uh(n) maidsa(n) eessee kee parl ah(n)glay?

Can you give me his address?

Pouvez-vous me donner son adresse?
Poovay-voo me(r) donnay soh(n) naddress?

What are the surgery hours?

Quelles sont les heures de consultation?
Kel soh(n) laze er de(r) coh(n)sewltassyoh(n)?

*There is no surgery today.

Il n'y a pas de consultation aujourd'hui.
Eel nyapah de(r) coh(n)sewltassyoh(n) ohzhoordwee.

Symptoms

My head aches.	**J'ai mal à la tête.**
	Zhay mal a la tet.
I ache all over.	**J'ai mal partout.**
	Zhay mal partoo.
I feel ...	**Je me sens ...**
	Zhe(r) me(r) sah(n) ...
– faint.	– **faible.**
	– febl.
– depressed.	– **déprimé.**
	– daypreemay.
– irritable.	– **irritable.**
	– eerreetahble.
– feverish.	– **fiévreux.**
	– fee-evre(r).
I feel dizzy.	**J'ai des vertiges.**
	Zhay day vairteezh.
I feel sick.	**J'ai mal au cœur.**
	Zhay mal oh ker.
I have been sick.	**J'ai eu des vomissements.**
	Zhay ew day vomeessmah(n).
I've got stomach-ache.	**J'ai mal au ventre.**
	Zhay mal oh vah(n)tr.
I've got diarrhoea.	**J'ai la diarrhée.**
	Zhay la deearray.
I am constipated.	**Je suis constipé.**
	Zhe(r) swee coh(n)steepay.
It hurts to pass water.	**Uriner me fait mal.**
	Youreenay me(r) fay mal.
I've got indigestion.	**J'ai une indigestion.**
	Zhay ewn a(n)deezhestyoh(n).
I've eaten something which did not agree with me.	**J'ai mangé quelque chose qui m'a fait mal.**
	Zhay mah(n)zhay kelke(r) shoze kee ma fay mal.
I have dreadful cramps.	**J'ai des crampes affreuses.**
	Zhay day crah(n)p zaffre(rz).

I have a bad cold.	**J'ai un grand rhume.** Zhay uh(n) grah(n) rewm.
I can't stop coughing/sneezing.	**Je tousse/éternue sans cesse.** Zhe(r) tooss/aytairnew sah(n) sess.
My eyes are watering.	**Mes yeux pleurent.** Maze ye(r) pler.
My vision is blurred/coloured.	**Ma vision est brouillée/colorée.** Ma veezyoh(n) ay brooeeyay/coloray.
I am seeing double.	**Je vois double.** Zhe(r) vwa doobl.
I've got something in my eye/ear.	**J'ai quelque chose dans l'œil/l'oreille.** Zhay kelke(r) shoze dah(n) le(r)j/loray.
The pain is ...	**La douleur est ...** La dooler ay ...
– acute.	**– aiguë.** – taygew.
– burning.	**– brûlante.** – brewlah(n)t.
– continuous.	**– continue.** – coh(n)teenyew.
– dull.	**– sourde.** – soord.
– intermittent.	**– intermittente.** – a(n)tairmeetah(n)t.
– throbbing.	**– lancinante.** – lah(n)sseenah(n)t.
– tight (pressing).	**– serrante.** – serrah(n)t.
– sharp.	**– vive.** – veev.
I have difficulty swallowing.	**J'ai du mal à avaler.** Zhay dew mal a avallay.

I have difficulty breathing.

Je respire avec peine.
Zhe(r) respeer avec pen.

I am having hot flushes.

J'ai des bouffées de chaleur.
Zhay day booffay de(r) shaller.

My glands are swollen.

J'ai les glandes gonflées.
Zhay lay glah(n)d goh(n)flay.

I have swallowed a lot of water.

J'ai avalé beaucoup d'eau.
Zhay avallay bohcoo doh.

I've lost the feeling in my arm.

J'ai le bras mort.
Zhay le(r) brah mor.

I've got a rash.

J'ai une éruptation.
Zhay ewn ayruptassyoh(n).

I can't get to sleep.

Je n'arrive pas à m'endormir.
Zhe(r) narreev pah a
mah(n)dormeer.

I have lost my appetite.

J'ai perdu mon appétit.
Zhay pairdew moh(n) nappaytee.

I fell over.

Je suis tombé par terre.
Zhe(r) swee tombay par tair.

I have banged my head.

Je me suis cogné la tête.
Zhe(r) me(r) swee conjay la tet.

My foot is swollen/numb.

J'ai le pied enflé/engourdi.
Zhay le(r) pyay ah(n)flay/
ah(n)goordee.

I have burnt my hand.

Je me suis brûlé la main.
Zhe(r) me(r) swee brewlay la
ma(n).

I have got sunstroke.

J'ai attrapé un coup de soleil.
Zhay attrappay uh(n) coo de(r)
solay.

I have been stung/bitten by a
jellyfish/sea urchin/snake/wasp/
flea/mosquito.

**Je me suis fait piquer par une
méduse/un oursin/un serpent/
une gûepe/une puce/un mostique.**
Zhe(r) me(r) swee fay peekay par
ewn mayduze/uh(n) oorsa(n)/
uh(n) sairpah(n)/ewn gwep/
ewn pewss/uh(n) moosteek.

I have been attacked by a dog.

J'ai été attaqué par un chien.
Zhay aytay attackay par uh(n) shyan.

Special conditions

I am allergic to penicillin.

Je suis allérgique à la pénicilline.
Zhe(r) sweez allairzheek a la payneesseeleen.

I am arthritic/asthmatic/diabetic/ epileptic.

Je suis arthritique/asthmatique/ diabetique/épileptique.
Zhe(r) sweez artreeteek/asmateek/ deeabayteek/aypeelepteek.

I have a heart condition.

Je suis cardiaque.
Zhe(r) swee cardiac.

I am expecting a baby in 5 months.

La naissance de mon enfant est pour dans cinq mois.
La naissah(n) de(r) moh(n) nah(n) fah(n) ay poor dah(n) sank mwa.

My child won't eat/drink anything.

Mon enfant ne veut pas manger/ boire.
Moh(n) nah(n)fah(n) ne(r) ve(r) pah mah(n)zhay/bwahr.

My baby won't stop crying.

Mon bébé ne cesse de pleurer.
Moh(n) baybay ne(r) sess de(r) pleray.

He doesn't seem well.

Il n'a pas l'air très bien.
Eel na pah lair tray bya(n).

Miscellaneous

I am taking pills regularly for . . . .

Je prends régulièrement des pilules pour . . . .
Zhe(r) prah(n) raygewlyairmah(n) day peelewl poor . . . .

I am on the pill.	**Je prends la pilule.** Zhe(r) prah(n) la peelewl.
I have lost/forgotten my pills/ medicine.	**J'ai perdu/oublié mes comprimés/ médicaments.** Zhay pairdew/ooblyay may coh(n)preemay/ maydeekamah(n).
Please can you give me a prescription for . . . ?	**Pouvez-vous me faire une ordonnance pour . . ., s'il vous plaît?** Poovay-voo me(r) fair ewn ordonah(n)ss poor . . ., seelvooplay?
Please can you inoculate me against . . . ?	**Pouvez-vous me vacciner contre . . ., s'il vous plaît?** Poovay-voo me(r) vakseenay coh(n)tr . . ., seelvooplay?

At the dentist's

Can you recommend a good dentist who speaks English?	**Pouvez-vous recommander un bon dentiste qui parle anglais?** Poovay-voo recommah(n)day uh(n) boh(n) dah(n)teest kee parl ah(n)glay?
I would like to make an appointment as soon as possible.	**Je voudrais avoir un rendez-vous le plus tôt possible.** Zhe(r) voodray avwahr uh(n) rah(n)day-voo le(r) plew toh posseebl.
I must see the dentist – it's urgent.	**Je dois voir le dentiste – c'est urgent.** Zhe(r) dwa vwahr le(r) dah(n)teest – say turzhah(n)t.

I have dreadful toothache.

J'ai très mal aux dents.
Zhay tray mal oh dah(n).

This tooth at the back/at the front/
on top/at the bottom/hurts.

**Cette dent derrière/devant/en
haut/en bas/me fait mal.**
Set dah(n) derryair/de(r)vah(n)/
ah(n) oh/ah(n) bah/me(r) fay
mal.

I have sore/swollen gums.

**J'ai les gencives douloureuses/
enflées.**
Zhay lay zhah(n)sseev
dooloore(r)z/ah(n)flay.

I have lost a filling.

J'ai perdu un plombage.
Zhay pairdew uh(n) plombahzh.

I have a loose filling/tooth.

**J'ai un plombage/une dent qui
remue.**
Zhay uh(n) plombahzh/ewn
dah(n) kee remew.

I have broken this tooth.

J'ai cassé cette dent.
Zhay cassay set dah(n).

I have false front teeth.

J'ai de fausses dents devant.
Zhay de(r) fohss dah(n)
de(r)vah(n).

I have broken/lost my dentures.

J'ai cassé/perdu mon dentier.
Zhay cassay/pairdew moh(n)
dah(n)tyay.

I think I am cutting a wisdom
tooth.

**Je crois que je perce une dent de
sagesse.**
Zhe(r) crwa ke(r) zhe(r) pairss
ewn dah(n) de(r) sazhess.

I am taking pills/medicine for ....

**Je prends régulièrement des
pilules/un médicament pour ....**
Zhe(r) prah(n)
raygewlyairmah(n) day
peelewl/uh(n)
maydeekamah(n) poor ....

I went to the dentist 2 weeks/
6 months/a year ago.

**Je suis allé chez le dentiste il y a
deux semaines/six mois/un an.**
Zhe(r) sweez allay shay le(r)
dah(n)teest eelya de(r) smen/
see mwa/uh(n) nah(n).

Accidents and Emergencies

Motorists can be fined on the spot by police for speeding and similar minor offences, and it is often easiest to pay up, or you could be involved in a court case.

If involved in an accident you should contact the police (**brigade de gendarmerie**) and obtain a written report (**procès verbal**) before the vehicle is moved. This is used as evidence in a court of law. Your insurance company should be notified within twenty-four hours.

The numbers for fire, police and ambulance services are given on the central telephone disc (see section on 'The Telephone').

There has been an accident.	**Il y a eu un accident.** Eelya ew uhnaksseedah(n).
Call a doctor/an ambulance/the police/the fire brigade.	**Appelez un médecin/une ambulance/la police/les pompiers.** Appellay uh(n) maidsa(n)/ewn ah(n)bewlah(n)ss/la poleess/lay poh(n)pyay.
Come quickly.	**Venez vite.** Venay veet.
There are several people hurt.	**Il y a plusieurs blessés.** Eelya plewzyer blessay.
It's very serious.	**C'est très grave.** Say tray grahv.
Don't move him/her until the doctor comes.	**Ne le/la bougez pas jusqu'à l'arrivée du médecin.** Ne(r) le(r)/la boozhay pah zhooska larreevay dew maidsa(n).

Is there anyone here who knows first aid?	**Y a-t-il quelqu'un ici qui sait donner les premiers secours?**
	Yateel kelkuh(n) eessee kee say donnay lay premyay sekoor?
Bring some blankets/bandages/a chair/some water.	**Apportez des couvertures/des bandages/une chaise/de l'eau.**
	Apportay day koovairtewr/day bah(n)dahzh/ewn shez/de(r) loh.
Does anyone speak English?	**Est-ce que quelqu'un parle anglais?**
	Esske(r) kelkuh(n) parl ah(n)glay?
Please can you help?	**Pouvez-vous aider, s'il vous plaît?**
	Poovay-voo zayday, seelvooplay?
Please give me your name and address.	**Donnez-moi votre nom et votre adresse, s'il vous plaît.**
	Donnay-mwa votr noh(n) ay votraddress, seelvooplay.
Here is my name and address.	**Voici mon nom et mon adresse.**
	Vwassee moh(n) noh(n) ay mohn address.
My husband is drowning.	**Mon mari se noie.**
	Moh(n) maree se(r) nwa.

Other awkward situations

My friend has been missing for	**Mon ami est absent depuis . . . .**
	Monamee ay tabsah(n) depwee . . . .
*When did you last see him?	**Quand l'avez-vous vu pour la dernière fois?**
	Kah(n) lavay-voo vew poor la dairnyer fwa?
*What was he wearing?	**Que portait-il?**
	Ke(r) portay-teel?

I think this child has lost his parents.

Je crois que cet enfant a perdu ses parents.

Zhe(r) crwa ke(r) set ah(n)fah(n) apairdew say parah(n).

My caravan is on fire.

Ma caravane a pris feu.

Ma caravahn a pree fe(r).

We were attacked in the woods.

On nous a attaqués dans les bois.

Oh(n) nooza attackay dah(n) lay bwa.

At the police station

I want to report an accident.

Je veux signaler un accident.

Zhe(r) ve(r) seenjalay uh(n) aksseedah(n).

My car has been in collision with a lorry.

Ma voiture est entrée en collision avec un camion.

Ma vwatewr ay tah(n)tray ah(n) kolleezyoh(n) avec uh(n) camyoh(n).

I crashed into a tree.

J'ai heurté un arbre.

Zhay ertay uh(n) arbr.

The other car didn't stop.

L'autre voiture ne s'est pas arrêtée.

Lohtr vwatewr ne(r) say pah zarretay.

He was travelling very fast.

Il allait très vite.

Eel allay tray veet.

I was travelling very slowly.

J'allais très lentement.

Zhallay tray lah(n)tmah(n).

Here is the registration number

Voici le numéro de la plaque d'immatriculation.

Vwassee le(r) newmairoh de(r) la plack deematreekewlassyoh(n).

Lost and stolen

I have lost ...	**J'ai perdu ...**
	Zhay pairdew ...
– my passport.	**– mon passeport.**
	– moh(n) passpor.
– my traveller's cheques.	**– mes chèques de voyage.**
	– may sheck de(r) vwa-yahzh.
– my car keys.	**– mes clefs de voiture.**
	– may klay de(r) vwatewr.
– my driving licence.	**– mon permis de conduire.**
	– moh(n) pairmee de(r) koh(n)dweer.
My car/hotel room has been burgled.	**On a cambriolé ma voiture/ma chambre d'hôtel.**
	Ohna kah(n)breeolay ma vwatyour/ma shah(n)br dohtel.
My camera has been stolen.	**On m'a volé mon appareil.**
	Oh(n) ma volay monapparay.
My suitcase ...	**– ma valise.**
	– ma valeez.
My car ...	**– ma voiture.**
	– ma vwatewr.
My wallet ...	**– mon porte-feuille.**
	– moh(n) portfe(r)y.
My money ...	**– mon argent.**
	– monarzhah(n).
My handbag ...	**– mon sac.**
	– moh(n) sak.
My jewellery ...	**– mes bijoux.**
	– may beezhoo.

Reference Section

Numbers

1	un, une uh(n), ewn		11	onze oh(n)z
2	deux de(r)		12	douze dooz
3	trois trwa		13	treize trayz
4	quatre katr		14	quatorze kattorz
5	cinq sank		15	quinze ka(n)z
6	six seess		16	seize sayz
7	sept set		17	dix-sept deess-set
8	huit weet		18	dix-huit deess-weet
9	neuf nerf		19	dix-neuf deess-nerf
10	dix deess		20	vingt va(n)

21	vingt et un va(n)-tay-uh(n)		27	vingt-sept va(n)-tset
22	vingt-deux va(n)-de(r)		28	vingt-huit va(n)-tweet
23	vingt-trois va(n)-trwa		29	vingt-neuf va(n)-tnerf
24	vingt-quatre va(n)-katr		30	trente trah(n)t
25	vingt-cinq va(n)-tsank		31	trente et un trah(n)-tay-uh(n)
26	vingt-six va(n)-tseess		32	trente-deux trah(n)t-de(r)

40	quarante karah(n)t
50	cinquante sankah(n)t
60	soixante swahssah(n)t
70	soixante-dix swahssah(n)t-deess
80	quatre-vingts katr-va(n)

90	quatre-vingt-dix katr-va(n)-deess
100	cent sah(n)
200	deux cents de(r)-sah(n)
250	deux cent cinquante de(r) sah(n) sankah(n)t
1000	mille meel

half	**la moitié**	la mwatyay
quarter	**le quart**	le(r) kahr
three-quarters	**trois-quarts**	trwa kahr
a few	**quelques**	kelke(r)
several	**plusieurs**	plewzyair
a little	**un peu**	uh(n) pe(r)
a lot, many	**beaucoup**	bohcoo
double	**double**	doobl
more	**plus**	plew
less	**moins**	mwa(n)

first	**premier, première**	pre(r)myay, pre(r)myair
second	**deuxième**	de(r)zyaym
third	**troisième**	trwazyaym
fourth	**quatrième**	katryaym
fifth	**cinquième**	sankyaym
sixth	**sixième**	seezyaym
seventh	**septième**	settyaym
eighth	**huitième**	weetyaym
ninth	**neuvième**	nervyaym
tenth	**dixième**	deezyaym
eleventh	**onzième**	oh(n)zyaym
twelfth	**douzième**	doozyaym
thirteenth	**treizième**	trayzyaym
fourteenth	**quatorzième**	kattorzyaym
fifteenth	**quinzième**	ka(n)zyaym
sixteenth	**seizième**	sayzyaym
seventeenth	**dix-septième**	deessettyaym
eighteenth	**dix-huitième**	dee-zweetyaym
nineteenth	**dix-neuvième**	dee-znervyaym
twentieth	**vingtième**	va(n)tyaym

once	**une fois**	ewn fwa
twice	**deux fois**	de(r) fwa
three times	**trois fois**	trwa fwa

Time

Days of the week

Monday	**lundi** luh(n)dee
Tuesday	**mardi** mardee
Wednesday	**mercredi** maircre(r)dee
Thursday	**jeudi** zhe(r)dee
Friday	**vendredi** vah(n)dre(r)dee
Saturday	**samedi** samdee
Sunday	**dimanche** deemah(n)sh

Months of the year

January	**janvier** zhah(n)vyay
February	**février** fevryay
March	**mars** marss
April	**avril** avreel
May	**mai** may
June	**juin** zhwa(n)
July	**juillet** zhweeyay
August	**août** oo
September	**septembre** septah(n)br
October	**octobre** octobr
November	**novembre** novah(n)br
December	**décembre** dayssah(n)br

The seasons

Spring	**le printemps** le(r) pra(n)tah(n)
Summer	**l'été** laytay
Autumn	**l'automne** lohton
Winter	**l'hiver** leevair

Telling the time

What is the time, please? **Quelle heure est-il, s'il vous plaît?**
Kel er ayteel, seelvooplay?

It is one o'clock/seven o'clock.	**Il est une heure/sept heures.**
	Eel ay tewn er/set er.
It is midday/midnight.	**Il est midi/minuit.**
	Eel ay meedee/meenwee.
It is a quarter past five/a quarter to six.	**Il est cinq heures et quart/six heures moins le quart.**
	Eel ay sank er ay kahr/see-zer mwa(n) le kahr.
It is half past two.	**Il est deux heures et demi**
	Eel ay de(r) zer ay de(r)mee
It is five past two/ten past three.	**Il est deux heures cinq/trois heures dix.**
	Eel ay de(r) zer sank/trwa zer deess.

Time phrases

today	**aujourd'hui** ohzhoordwee
this morning	**ce matin** se(r) matta(n)
this afternoon	**cet après-midi** set apray-meedee
this evening	**ce soir** se(r) swahr
tonight	**cette nuit** set nwee
this week	**cette semaine** set smen
this month	**le mois courant** le(r) mwa coorah(n)
tomorrow	**demain** de(r)ma(n)
the day after tomorrow	**le lendemain** le(r) lah(n)de(r)ma(n)
next week	**la semaine prochaine** la smen proshen
next month	**le mois prochain** le(r) mwa prosha(n)
yesterday	**hier** yair
the day before yesterday	**avant-hier** avah(n)-tyair
last week	**la semaine dernière** la se(r)mayn dairnyair
last month	**le mois dernier** le(r) mwa dairnyay
now	**maintenant** ma(n)te(r)nah(n)
soon	**bientôt** bya(n)toh
in five minutes	**dans cinq minutes** dah(n) sa(n) meenewt

in an hour	**dans une heure**	dah(n) zewn er
in a few days	**dans quelques jours**	dah(n) kelke(r) zhoor
one day	**un jour**	uh(n) zhoor
early	**de bonne heure**	de(r) bon er
earlier	**de plus bonne heure**	de(r) plew bon er
late	**tard**	tar
later	**plus tard**	plew tar
never	**jamais**	zhammay
this year	**cette année**	set annay
next year	**l'année prochaine**	lannay proshen
last year	**l'année dernière**	lannay dairnyair

Public holidays in France

1 January	New Year's Day
1 May	Labour Day
14 July	Bastille Day
15 August	Feast of the Assumption
1 November	All Saints' Day
11 November	Armistice Day 1918
25 December	Christmas Day

Conversion tables

INCHES TO CENTIMETRES

in	in or cm	cm
0.394	1	2.540
0.787	2	5.080
1.181	3	7.620
1.575	4	10.160
1.169	5	12.700
2.362	6	15.240
2.756	7	17.780
3.150	8	20.320
3.543	9	22.860
3.937	10	25.400
7.874	20	50.800
9.843	25	63.500
19.685	50	127.000
39.370	100	254.000

YARDS TO METRES

yd	yd or m	m
1.094	1	0.914
2.187	2	1.829
3.281	3	2.743
4.374	4	3.658
5.468	5	4.572
6.562	6	5.486
7.655	7	6.401
8.749	8	7.315
9.843	9	8.230
10.936	10	9.144
21.872	20	18.288
27.340	25	22.860
54.681	50	45.720
109.361	100	91.439
546.805	500	457.195

MILES TO KILOMETRES

miles	miles or km	km
0.621	1	1.609
1.242	2	3.218
1.864	3	4.827
2.485	4	6.437
3.107	5	8.046
3.728	6	9.655
4.350	7	11.265
4.971	8	12.874
5.592	9	14.483
6.214	10	16.093
15.535	25	40.232
31.070	50	80.465
46.605	75	120.696
62.136	100	160.930
124.272	200	321.860
186.408	300	382.790
310.680	500	804.650

POUNDS TO KILOGRAMMES

lb	lb or kg	kg
2.205	1	0.453
4.409	2	0.907
6.614	3	1.360
8.818	4	1.814
11.023	5	2.268
13.228	6	2.721
15.432	7	3.175
17.637	8	3.628
19.841	9	4.082
22.046	10	4.435
44.092	20	9.071
55.116	25	11.339
110.232	50	22.680
220.464	100	45.359

POUNDS PER SQUARE INCH TO KILOGRAMMES PER SQUARE CENTIMETRE

lb/in²	kg/cm²
18	1.266
20	1.406
22	1.547
25	1.758
29	2.039
32	2.250
35	2.461
36	2.531
39	2.742
40	2.812

GALLONS TO LITRES

gal	l or gal	l
0.22	1	4.55
0.44	2	9.09
0.66	3	13.64
0.88	4	18.18
1.10	5	22.73
1.32	6	27.28
1.54	7	31.83
1.76	8	36.37
1.98	9	40.91
2.20	10	45.46
4.40	20	90.92
6.60	30	136.38
8.80	40	181.84
11.00	50	227.30
16.50	75	340.95
22.00	100	454.59
33.00	150	681.89

TEMPERATURE: FAHRENHEIT AND CENTIGRADE

°F	°C	
−22	−30	
−4	−20	
+14	−10	
+23	−5	
+32	0	
+41	+5	
+50	+10	
+68	+20	
+85	+30	normal
+98.4	+36.9	body
+104	+40	temperature
+122	+50	
+140	+60	
+157	+70	
+176	+80	
+194	+90	
+212	+100	

Index

FRENCH

J. ADAMS and N. SCARLYN WILSON

This book has been specially written with the needs of the beginner studying at home in mind. No knowledge of the language is assumed and every stage is fully illustrated with examples and exercises. Pronunciation, grammar and syntax are comprehensively covered and the book will give you a basic, everyday vocabulary.

TEACH YOURSELF BOOKS

FRENCH GRAMMAR

E. S. JENKINS

This book aims to present clearly and concisely the basic rules of French grammar which must be mastered by all who want to speak and translate French fluently. It is intended for revision and quick reference, and assumes that the reader already knows the basics of French grammar from working through a course such as FRENCH in the Teach Yourself series.

'An excellent book for examination revision if only for the clarity of its layout and the multiplicity of well chosen French examples.'

The Times Literary Supplement

TEACH YOURSELF BOOKS

FRENCH DICTIONARY

This dictionary provides the user with a comprehensive vocabulary for working French, containing over 35,000 words in both sections. Special emphasis has been placed on current usage and some slang has been included. A complete list of irregular verbs, a selection of French idioms and phrases, lists of Christian names and geographical places are all included. This extensive and workmanlike dictionary will prove invaluable to the student of French.

TEACH YOURSELF BOOKS

EVERYDAY FRENCH

N. SCARLYN WILSON

This book is designed for the student who can already read and write basic French and wishes to consolidate and extend his knowledge of the modern language. Sections on idiomatic usage, conversational, commercial and literary French—all fully illustrated with examples—are provided with the aim of giving practical help to the reader in capturing the living spirit of the language.

TEACH YOURSELF BOOKS